# All My Octobers

MY MEMORIES OF
TWELVE WORLD
SERIES WHEN
THE YANKEES
RULED
BASEBALL

# MICKEY MANTLE

WITH MICKEY HERSKOWITZ

HARPER

NEW YORK ● LONDON ● TORONTO ● SYDNEY

*In loving memory of my son Billy*

HARPER

A hardcover edition of this book was published in 1994 by HarperCollins Publishers.

HarperCollins books may be purchased for educational, business, or sales promotional use. For information please write: Special Markets Department, HarperCollins Publishers, 10 East 53rd Street, New York, NY 10022.

First Harper paperback published 2006.

*Designed by Nancy Singer*

The Library of Congress has catalogued the hardcover edition as follows:

Mantle, Mickey, 1931-1995.
    All my Octobers: my memories of 12 World Series when the Yankees ruled baseball / Mickey Mantle with Mickey Herskowitz.—1st ed.
      p. cm.
    Includes index.
    ISBN 0-06-017747-0
    1. World Series (Baseball)—History. 2. New York Yankees (Baseball team)—History. I. Herskowitz, Mickey. II. Title
GV878.4.M35 1994
796.357'646—dc20                            94-8578

ISBN-10: 0-06-113172-5 (pbk.)
ISBN-13: 978-0-06-113172-1 (pbk.)

06 07 08 09 10 RRD 10 9 8 7 6 5 4 3 2 1

# CONTENTS

Photographs follow page 128.

# ACKNOWLEDGMENTS

I have a lot of people to thank for their time and support and memories, and helping me relive my World Series years and turn them into a book.

I want to start with Hank Bauer, Moose Skowron, Enos Slaughter, Yogi Berra, Johnny Blanchard, Tommy Tresh, Jake Gibbs, Ron Guidry, Bobby Murcer, and Catfish Hunter. They were my teammates long ago and, as far as I'm concerned, my teammates still. They join me the last week of October every year for Mickey Mantle's "Week of Dreams" in Fort Lauderdale, Florida. We talked about the book, and worked on it there last fall.

Yogi and I have a kind of trade-off. He not only coaches at the camps when he can, we play in each other's golf tournaments: his in New Jersey for the Boy Scouts, and mine for the Make a Wish Foundation at Shangri La, in Oklahoma, near Spavinaw.

I've actually turned the management of my fantasy camps over to my sons, Mickey, Jr., David, Billy, and Danny. So they're my "bosses" now, along with a couple of friends, Mike and Wanda Greer.

Some of my old foes were kind enough to be interviewed and shared their recollections, among them: Johnny Podres, Carl Erskine, Ralph Branca, Johnny Rutherford, Bobby Thomson, Monte Irvin, Alvin Dark, Lew Burdette, Dick Groat, Andy Pafko, Orlando Cepeda, Tim

McCarver. I thank them, and all the great teams and great years they represented.

Dave Pietrusza of SABR (the Society of American Baseball Researchers) spent many hours assisting with these interviews.

Rob Butcher, of the Yankees media relations staff, and Bill Burdick, of the Baseball Hall of Fame, were generous in combing through photo files for many of the pictures that appear in these pages. Thanks are also owed to Larry Keith, the special projects editor at *Sports Illustrated*, and his assistant, Rick Lipsey.

Mike Olson and Rod Harris of Toshiba's computer services took some of the worry out of the technical side. Terry Diehl, of the library staff of the *Houston Post*, helped check the dates and facts.

Finally, and yet up at the top of the list, I owe thanks to the whole crew at HarperCollins, Gladys Justin Carr, Cynthia Barrett, Elissa Altman, Tracy Devine, and Pamela LaBarbiera for their ideas, their encouragement, and their understanding. I've found that publishing a book has this in common with baseball: it's a long season.

# INTRODUCTION

## BOB COSTAS, NBC SPORTS

It's a 1958 Mickey Mantle All-Star card, part of a series the Topps Company printed as an addition to their official regular-season sets. The All-Star card has a red background, with a full-length photo of Mantle swinging right-handed and surrounded by a ring of gold stars.

It was one of hundreds, if not thousands, of cards I kept in a shoe box that year. I was six years old. From then on, I collected cards every year until I was twelve. Nobody considered baseball cards an investment then. You sorted them, flipped them, traded them, put them on the spokes of your bike to make a very cool sound as you pedaled around the neighborhood (a Willie Tasby was more likely to be used for this purpose than a Willie Mays). But monetary value? Hell, you got five of them in a pack, plus a piece of gum, for a nickel!

I stopped collecting cards around 1965. Didn't even protest when my mom tossed out the shoe box and its contents sometime later. But I did have the presence of mind to pull that Mantle card from the stack before the rest (such as the Eli Grbas and Bob Purkeys) had their rendezvous with the incinerator. I slipped it in my wallet, and over the years, whenever I got a new billfold, I just transferred it along with my driver's license and credit cards. It would have seemed almost a sacrilege to throw it away.

No one said anything about it until I had broken into baseball broadcasting with NBC. Then Tony Kubek mentioned the card on baseball's *Game of the Week,* and had me show it on camera. In the mid-eighties, a story in *Sports Illustrated* made a point of referring to it.

From then on, I lost track of the number of times people asked me, "Do you have the Mantle card? Can I see that Mantle card?" I always have it. I do not ascribe any spiritual qualities to it, but I am never without it. It's a connection to my childhood—when baseball meant nearly everything to me, and Mantle was as much a symbol of baseball as Cracker Jacks.

I grew up in New York, a Yankee fan from the age of five. The Dodgers and Giants had just played their last seasons in New York. I was ten when the Mets came into existence. So during that period, when your baseball sensibilities take shape and you really become familiar with the game, the Yankees were the only team in New York, the only team on the air.

The Yankees televised more than one hundred games a year, including every home game, so I developed a very strong mental image of Mantle by the time I was six years old. It starts out as an image in black and white. It is an image from behind home plate. The center-field camera didn't come in until many years later, so all the standard shots were slightly elevated and from behind the batter. I remember Mantle kneeling in the on-deck circle, that broad back, with the number 7 and the pinstripes. No one kneels in the on-deck circle anymore. I wonder if Andy Rooney has noticed that?

On television, when a fly ball was hit to him, Mantle was framed by the monuments in center field, with the flagpole rising up behind them. Even to a six- or seven-year-old kid, Yankee Stadium seemed so much more classic than the places where they would play on the road.

Obviously Fenway Park and Tiger Stadium have great histories, but if you saw Mantle playing in Kansas City, that literally seemed off-Broadway. It was partly because of New York, mostly because of Yankee Stadium. The majesty of that setting wasn't lost, even on a kid.

My first trip to Yankee Stadium was a visit to hallowed ground. It was the last week of the 1959 season, one of only two years in a span of twelve when they didn't win the pennant. I was amazed by how vivid the colors were—I had never seen the Stadium in anything but black and white.

When I first walked in, I was struck by the brightness of the grass, the brownish orange of the cinder track, and how white and clean the bases were. The feeling was not unlike watching *The Wizard of Oz,* when the scene changes from the black and white of Kansas to the vibrant color of Oz. I walked up that ramp and all of a sudden the vista opened up and I saw the field spreading out in front of me. Everything looked different, particularly the dimensions. The technology of television couldn't capture the size of it, or the spatial relations—how far apart the players stood from each other—especially in a park with an outfield as huge as Yankee Stadium's. To a seven-year-old, it seemed like the biggest, most dramatic, most important place on earth.

Mantle did not play that day. Johnny Blanchard hit a home run, but the Yankees lost, 7-2. My disappointment at not seeing Mantle play was partly offset by literally tracing his steps. The fans used to be able to exit the ballpark by cutting across the ball field, so I followed my father onto the field and ran to the spot where Mick had made so many of his catches. Then I headed to the power alley in right center, where so many of his home runs had cleared the fence and gone into the bleachers. After that, we got out to dead center field, where the monuments were, 460 feet or more from home plate. From the perspective of a seven-year-old kid, I couldn't see home plate. The top of the pitcher's mound loomed like the crest of a hill. I thought, How can anyone hit a ball out here, or throw a ball from here to the infield? I made all the players, especially Mantle, the best and the mightiest, that much larger than life.

The first World Series I followed closely was in 1960, when the Yankees met the Pirates. All the games were in the daytime, so, except for weekend games, if you went to school you missed the Series. I took a transistor radio, listened when I could, and got the reports that always filtered through school.

That was a great shared bit of growing up that kids don't have today. Listening to the World Series was like having an unofficial holiday. The Yankees were always in it. If you had the right teacher, one who liked baseball, he or she might bring a television set into the classroom, and you sat there and watched the game. It felt like a hundred Saturdays strung together, watching a game in your classroom. All the formality and best-behavior pretense of school now had given way to a ball game.

Still, I refused to even go to school on the days of the sixth and seventh games. I didn't want to miss a pitch. My parents were truly enlightened—they understood and let me stay home.

The Yankees were so clearly superior to the Pirates that it seemed absurd to me that the Series had gone to a seventh game. The Yanks fell behind, 4-0, then came back to go in front, 7-4. I figured they had done this for theatrical purposes, but when a sure double-play ball bad-hopped wildly and smacked Tony Kubek in the throat at shortstop, the door was opened for a five-run Pittsburgh eighth. So the Yanks were down 9-7 going to the top of the ninth. As I held my breath, Mantle had a big hit in a two-run rally that tied it again, 9-9.

Then Bill Mazeroski won the game and the Series with his homer in the bottom of the ninth. I can still see the ball clearing the ivy-covered wall at Forbes Field, Yogi Berra looking on helplessly. I went to my room and cried for what seemed like an hour. It might have been fifteen minutes. Then I refused to speak, an act of willpower for me, even at the age of eight. At dinner, after describing every detail of the game, I told my mother and father that I wasn't going to speak again until the next baseball season started.

My protest ended the next morning on the school bus, as I responded to the ignorant taunts of a Yankee-hating dolt who actually contended that the Bombers were inferior to the Bucs, rather than victims of a comic injustice. As Mickey relates in Chapter 8, he too regards 1960 as his most bitter World Series memory, despite his three homers and .400 average in the Classic.

That was the first of five World Series appearances for the Yankees to open the decade, and, as it turned out, to close the Yankee dynasty that had lasted four decades.

I recall all those fall afternoons of thirty-plus years ago more vividly than last year's World Series, or the one the year before. This might seem strange to non-baseball fans, but perfectly natural to those who grew up with the game and loved it unconditionally, in an era, and at an age, when there was much less competition for our attention and affection. The win over the Reds in 1961, with Mantle missing most of the Series with an abscessed hip. Bobby Richardson clutching Willie McCovey's wicked liner to end the seventh game with the Giants in 1962 (a series in which neither Mantle nor Mays excelled). Sandy Koufax's mastery of the Yanks in the Dodgers' sweep a year later, although Mantle did go deep on him in Game 4. That homer tied Babe Ruth's World Series mark and set the stage for Mickey's record-breaking sixteenth World Series homer in Game 3 in 1964 against St. Louis. I can still hear the crack of the bat as Mantle sent a Barney Shultz knuckler crashing into the upper deck at Yankee Stadium. Well, you get the idea.

I ran into Mick once sitting in a restaurant with Billy

Crystal, and they waved me over. Billy grew up on Long Island, a rabid and knowledgeable Yankee fan, so he and I regaled Mickey with recollections of specific games and situations well into the night. A homer over the roof in Detroit. A surprise drag bunt in Baltimore. Mickey laughed and sometimes shook his head at the obscure details we not only remembered, but still savored.

Such sessions, I think, did something valuable for Mickey. There are so many millions who recognize him, who feel they know him, who constantly ask for autographs and pictures, that it is almost numbing. It is impossible for a person to respond in kind to all that. But when he can put a name or a face to it, as with Billy Crystal and me, the years come alive again. We represent all the kids who grew up rooting for Mickey Mantle

Here we are in our forties now, with other things in our lives. We are not professional collectors, not Rotisserie League addicts, nothing like that. We probably don't even like baseball as much as we once did. Yet he still means something to us. I hope he feels good about that.

Mickey is quick to say he shouldn't have been presented as a role model. He is right. But if he thinks he wasn't a hero, he is wrong. I've got a thirty-six-year-old bubble gum card that says he was—and always will be.

Bob Costas will provide the play-by-play for NBC's baseball telecasts in 1994, and with Bob Uecker forms the network's #1 broadcasting team.

# WOUNDED KNEE

## 1951—YANKEES 4, GIANTS 2

Branch Rickey once said that to play baseball it was neces-
sary only to have a ball, a bat, a glove, and the imagination
of a young boy. By the time I was five I had them all. My
dad whittled his broken bats down to my size, and he
pitched to me every day if there was daylight left when he
got home from working in the zinc mines.

On weekends, Dad played semipro ball. He could run,
pitch, field any position, hit for power, and had the best
arm in Oklahoma—at least in my eyes. The scouts never
saw him play.

All of my early memories about the World Series are
woven around my family and glad times laced by pain and
sadness. That became a kind of pattern of mine and I never
questioned my luck, good or bad. I was just a mouse in a
maze; I'd get the cheese and then the electric shock.
Ballplayers were always saying that over the long term the

breaks evened out. But not everybody hangs around for the long term.

The first World Series I can clearly remember paired the St. Louis Cardinals and the Boston Red Sox, in 1946; Stan Musial against Ted Williams. I was turning fifteen, a sophomore in high school, and I listened to Harry Caray's play-by-play on the radio beside my bed in the Crippled Children's Hospital in Oklahoma City. I was being treated for osteomyelitis, an infection in the bone marrow caused, in my case, by a kick in the shin during a high school football practice. My leg had started to turn purple, my ankle was so swollen it was bigger than my knee, and I was running a fever, as high as 104.

I had no way of knowing then that I would have leg problems the rest of my life, which for most of my years meant baseball.

I had been examined at the hospital closest to our home in Commerce, and the doctor warned my mother they might have to amputate the leg. She said, "Like hell you will," and yanked me out of there. We made the 175-mile drive to Oklahoma City, where the hospital had a large staff and, of more importance, accepted patients who couldn't pay. I was stretched out in the back seat of our beat-up 1935 LaSalle. All the way there I worried about never playing baseball again, and I felt for my dad because I knew how much pride Elvin "Mutt" Mantle had to choke down to accept charity.

Around this time a wonder drug called penicillin had become widely available. I had an injection every three hours around the clock and began to improve almost immediately. To continue the good news, Enos Slaughter scored from first base on a hit by Harry "The Hat" Walker to win the seventh game and the World Series for St. Louis. Commerce was in northeast Oklahoma, ten miles from the Missouri state line, and we Mantles were Cardinal fans. I remember my dad taking me to a Class C baseball game, Joplin against Springfield, and pointing to a young player hitting line drives during batting practice. "See that guy?" he said. "He's going to be a major league star." He was pointing to Stan Musial.

While my mother washed and ironed the clothes, she always had a yellow writing tablet near the ironing board. She kept score off the radio. When my dad came home from the mines, close to nightfall, she could tell him everything he missed.

A scout named Tom Greenwade signed me to a Yankees' contract on the day I graduated from high school when I was seventeen. I was a shortstop then, an erratic one, and Greenwade sort of emphasized that I was a risk. He offered me $400 to play the rest of that summer at Independence, then closed the deal with a bonus of $1,100. But I learned much later that he paid me a compliment that couldn't be measured in dollars. After watching me play, he told the Yankees' brass: "Now I know how Paul Krichell must have felt the first time he saw Lou Gehrig."

Two years later—and five years after I heard Harry Caray describe Slaughter's mad dash from first—I played for the New York Yankees in the first World Series I ever saw. The year was 1951 and, to this day, the memory is still strange and mixed and unreal to me. When I was a boy there was nothing in sports, and not much anywhere else, that so demanded your interest. The Kentucky Derby did— for about two minutes. The biggest show in football was the Rose Bowl. Pro basketball hadn't yet found an audience, and most of the teams played in ratty old gyms.

But the week of the World Series, teachers would let you bring portable radios to school—they were about the size of a toaster—or even excuse classes early so you could rush home and hear the broadcasts.

At the movies in late October, the newsreels would show highlights from the Series, with the announcer describing the action over the crowd noise. In every reel, it seemed Joe DiMaggio would be getting a hit and running to first. Between features, they ran what they called "shorts."

Robert Benchley would do a bit about how hard it was to take a nap, and there was always a scene at the zoo, ending with Pete Smith saying, "Monkeys are the cwaziest people."

Baseball was a smaller and more orderly world then. There were eight teams in each major league, and there were no designated hitters, no artificial turf, no domed stadiums. But the fundamental rules never changed. If you got three strikes, not even Clarence Darrow could get you off.

Of all sports baseball has the longest season, and the reason you suffered through it (besides the money, which wasn't great in the 1950s) was to win the World Series. That may sound like corn, but it was pure American corn. You could ask any player, then or now, and he would give the same answer.

Anytime the Yankees made it that far and lost, they felt as if they had failed. It was like getting a silver medal in the Olympics. What that means is, of all the losers in all the world you're the best.

The first official World Series was played in 1903, when the Boston Pilgrims (later the Red Sox) of the new American League upset the Pittsburgh Pirates. The Yankees didn't win their first pennant until 1921. Between that appearance and my last in 1964, the Yankees were in the World Series twenty-nine times in forty-four years. That is just a wipeout performance. I was in a dozen of those, on the winning side in seven.

Given those opportunities, I broke Babe Ruth's record for most home runs (18), and wound up with the records for runs batted in (40), runs scored (42), walks (43), and, yes, strikeouts (54). Yet I never felt I played as well as I was able, never had what I considered a totally dominating Series.

It seemed as if I was always getting injured or playing with an old hurt. And too often I felt, when I got big hits or played at my peak, it wasn't enough and the team lost. I never thought the fans saw the best of Number 7 in the fall classic.

I had a kind of complex about it right from the start. We were playing the New York Giants, who had beaten the Dodgers on Bobby Thomson's home run in the most historic of all pennant races. That one was the Mona Lisa. The Yankees had caught Cleveland to clinch first place in the American League in the final week. I was on the bench for the two games that decided it, as Casey Stengel went with his veterans. Allie Reynolds assured us of a tie by beating the Red Sox on his second no-hitter of the season. The next day, Vic Raschi beat them for his twenty-first win and Joe DiMaggio hit a three-run homer, his 361st, and his last in regular season play.

I had been shipped back to the minors at mid-season, played well in September, but didn't really feel I belonged in the company of DiMaggio, Bauer, Berra, Rizzuto, and the rest.

Willie Mays and I were both rookies that year and went through pretty much the same kind of trials. The Giants called up Willie from Minneapolis in May and he went hitless his first twenty-four times at bat. He actually broke down and cried and begged Leo Durocher to send him down. Then, in a game the Giants would lose to Warren Spahn and the Braves, Willie hit his first home run. Years later, Bob Creamer would write in *Sports Illustrated*: "The crowd leaped up and roared and cheered as though Willie had just won the World Series. It was a strange, tingly thing to be a part of, because all that the crowd was saying really was, 'Welcome, Willie, we've been waiting all our lives for you.' "

We kept an eye on each other, Willie and me.

I gave some hard thought to quitting baseball when I was struggling at Kansas City, the Yankees' Triple-A farm club. After I whimpered to my dad about how tough things were, he drove five hours from Commerce and announced he was there to help me pack. Started throwing my things into a suitcase. Told me I could work in the mines the rest of my life, like him. That was all the encouragement I needed.

Coming out of spring training, Casey Stengel had convinced the front office to keep me with the big club. I was making the jump from Class C, and Casey told the press: "There's never been anyone like this kid which we got from Joplin. He has more speed than any slugger and more slug than any speedster—and nobody has ever had more of both of them together."

The buildup took on a life of its own, and the fans in New York thought they were getting a combination of Babe Ruth and Joe DiMaggio. All they really got was a scared nineteen-year-old kid who didn't know anything.

The 1951 season was the last for DiMaggio, the player I consider the best all-around in history. But it's no secret I wasn't comfortable around him. My locker was next to his, but I thought it would be out of line for me to speak to him first. As a result, we hardly spoke at all the entire season.

I realize now that I should have asked Joe to help me in some way. I think he would have liked that, and we might have become friends. Instead, even to this day, there is still a time-wall between us. The few times each year our paths cross, the talk is polite but brief.

I don't know if the Giants were still in a daze after coming from thirteen and a half games behind to catch the Dodgers, or if we had the better club. All I know is that, for me, the '51 Series was short and ironic. My career almost ended right there, in Game 2, on a play involving DiMaggio and Willie Mays.

When I have described this incident in the past, I sometimes softened it. But this is what really happened. DiMaggio had been in pain most of the season from a sore Achilles tendon. I was starting in right field and Casey told me to take anything I could reach. "The big Dago's heel is hurting pretty bad," is the way he put it.

For the opening-day ceremonies at Yankee Stadium they had a lot of what passes for fanfare in baseball—a marching band, Al Schacht's clown act, and the orchestra of Guy Lombardo and the Royal Canadians. The Giants beat us, 5-1, with their fourth starter, Dave Koslo. I led off and went hitless. The other rookie in our lineup, second baseman Gil McDougald, had a double and scored our only run. The Giants pounded Allie Reynolds for ten hits, including a three-run homer by Alvin Dark in the sixth inning. They scored twice in the first inning and embarrassed us when Monte Irvin stole home—that hadn't been done in a World Series since 1921. The last time the Yankees had lost the opener of a World Series was in 1936, when DiMaggio was a rookie.

We tied the Series with a win in the second game, 3-1, behind lefty Ed Lopat. I was determined to get a hit and I did it with a drag bunt past the pitcher, Larry Jansen, in the first inning. Rizzuto beat out another bunt and McDougald singled to right and I scored our first run. In the bottom of the second, Joe Collins homered into the seats in right field, the only extra base hit of the game.

We were ahead 2-0, but I wasn't around to see the finish. In the fifth inning, Mays led off for the Giants and popped a fly ball into short right-center. I knew there was no way DiMaggio could get to it so I hauled ass. Just as I arrived, I heard Joe say, "I got it!" I looked over and he was *camped* under the ball. I put on the brakes and the spikes on my right shoe caught the rubber cover of a sprinkler head. There was a sound like a tire blowing out and my right knee collapsed. I fell to the ground and stayed there, motionless. A bone was sticking out the side of my leg. DiMaggio leaned over me and said, "Don't move. They're bringing a stretcher."

I guess that was about as close as Joe and I had come to a conversation. I don't know what impressed me more, the injury or the sight of an aging DiMaggio still able to make a difficult catch look easy.

The next morning my dad and I caught a cab to the

Lenox Hill Hospital to have my knee operation. When we stepped out of the cab, I put my weight on his shoulder to support myself and he just crumpled to the ground. That was the first indication I had that my father was dying.

We wound up in the same hospital room, me recovering from surgery on my torn ligaments and my dad undergoing a battery of tests. He was a proud, rugged, sturdy man, six-two and two hundred pounds, and I thought not even the mines could beat him down. He had been coughing up black mucous for years. There was nearly always a cigarette hanging from his lip and he didn't believe in doctors. When he arrived in New York for the Series, I was shocked at his appearance. He looked pale and gaunt and his khaki pants were hanging on him. He must have lost thirty pounds.

My dad was out of the room and I was watching one of the games on television when a doctor walked in. His voice was so low I could barely understand him. "Your father is dying of Hodgkin's disease," he said. "Nothing can be done. Take him home and let him enjoy the time he has left." Hodgkin's is a form of cancer that atttacks the lymph nodes and eventually destroys the bone marrow.

I didn't suspect, or didn't want to suspect, how grave his condition was. I knew he was losing weight and stooped over, but I thought that was part of just getting older. That's how naive I was. He was forty-one when he died the following May. No male in the Mantle family had lived longer.

I see no reason to recycle my life story. I told it once, in 1985, in a book called *The Mick* (with Herb Gluck). But here's the short version: I was born on October 20, 1931, the oldest of five kids, four boys and a girl; the twins, Ray and Roy, my sister, Barbara, and the youngest brother, Butch.

By the time I was thirteen, my grandpa Charlie and my two uncles, Tunney and Emmett, had died of Hodgkin's. I took it for granted that I would not live to see forty.

As a five- or six-year-old, I would stand in the front yard watching the cars and trucks go by with people jammed in and water jugs banging against the sides. They were all heading the same way—west. In the summer, nights following the days, we slept with a wet washrag over our faces to filter the dust.

Those were the Dust Bowl days and the state was being stripped of its riches. The Mantles stayed put, but the term "Okies" became a slur that scarred an entire state. There is something pretty unjust when a whole group of people are made to feel inferior when all they wanted was enough honest work to live on.

My dad graded roads and tried farming, but he always came back to the mines. Wherever we called home, he marked off an area where we could play ball. I'm not bragging, but I was born to be a big leaguer. My dad had it all figured out. He was a St. Louis fan, but he named me after his favorite player, Mickey Cochrane, the hard-nosed, hard-hitting catcher for the Detroit Tigers. Dad thought that would be a fine baseball player's name—Mickey Mantle. It always sounded good to me.

Of course, the best baseball name ever invented was Babe Ruth. And just as summer follows spring, I was expected to follow DiMaggio in the line of succession that went back to the Babe.

Baseball became more than fun, more than a way out of the mines. I would turn twenty three weeks after the 1951 World Series, and I knew then that it would enable me to support my family, and provide the comforts my father could never afford.

I celebrated my birthday in a cast after my surgery. That was the first of five knee operations I would require. I wouldn't play another game the rest of my career without hurting. I had myself to blame mostly. I didn't do the exercises or lift the weights the doctors told me I needed in the off-season. Once I tossed aside my crutches, that was the end of my therapy. I can't explain why. Just young and stubborn and foolish.

The Yankees crossed the Harlem River the next day and lost at the Polo Grounds, 6-3, then won three in a row to take the Series in six games. DiMaggio hit the last homer of his career in Game 4 off Sal Maglie, and McDougald had a grand slam in Game 5 off Jansen.

I had not been a factor and neither was Willie Mays, who played in every game and hit just .182. A bad experience for both of us. But I learned quickly how contrary the baseball fates can be. I would hate to figure what the odds were that Joe DiMaggio and Willie Mays would be involved in the single play that nearly ended my career before it had begun to bloom.

In 1993 each Philadelphia Phillies player received a check for over $91,000 for losing the Series. In 1951 that wouldn't have missed by much of covering the winning shares for the entire Yankee team. As it was, I collected $6,445 for my first World Series share, which almost matched my salary. That was found money, and it helped me do three things. I bought a neat, seven-room house for my mom and dad, at 317 South River Street in Commerce. We even had our own phone. I didn't have to work again in the mines as I had the previous winter. And two days after Christmas I married Merlyn Johnson, who had been a majorette at a school in a nearby small Oklahoma town when we met and fell in love. I gave her an engagement ring with a quarter-carat diamond that cost $250. I had a lot of growing up still ahead of me, but I had begun to put aside my boyhood.

I know my father was happy about my marrying Merlyn. On his trip to New York, he had gotten a glimpse of how friendly some of the showgirls were and he was kind of worried about me. He told me if I was serious about Merlyn I needed to marry her, "because I want a redheaded grandson." We gave him four, Mickey Jr., David, Billy, and

Danny, but he didn't live to see any of them.

That winter, Merlyn and I drove my dad to the Mayo Clinic in Rochester, Minnesota, to see if they could help him. They gave him medication that eased his pain, but there was nothing anyone could do to cure him. We brought him home to Commerce, and a few weeks later he decided to go out to Denver, where one of the hospitals had a treatment he thought he should try.

I believed just about anything in those days, but I know now that he just didn't want his family to see him wasting away, getting thinner and sicker. I thought then that he was the bravest man I ever knew, and nothing has happened over the years to change my mind.

He had a big presence and an even temper, but he would get what I called quiet mad. I have a childhood memory of a barn dance, where all the families in town showed up, including kids. A couple of wise guys started to make trouble for the usual reason, just to show how mean and stupid they could be. They started to ruin the evening for everybody, then suddenly the unpleasantness passed. My uncles told me later that my father took the two troublemakers outside and whipped them both. Just like that. No fuss. No bother. They left and he went back inside and the dance went on. It became one of those stories that people liked to tell when they were sitting around, talking about the old days. My father never mentioned it.

The story has nothing to do with the Yankees winning the World Series in 1951, of course. But it had a lot to do with the making of Mickey Charles Mantle.

DiMaggio made his retirement official after the Series, ending any doubt when he said, simply, "I'm not Joe DiMaggio anymore." Everyone knew what he meant, but it didn't lessen the sadness the fans felt in New York and across the country.

I guess it is the nature of the game that each World Series is often identified with a certain player, a hit, a catch, a performance. In my mind, 1951 will always remind me of

DiMaggio. For as little as we have known each other he cast a wide shadow over my career.

I never felt that I was competing with the record Joe left behind, and I certainly didn't compare myself to him. I do believe that near the end of my time, my teammates had a feeling for me close to what the Yankees of Joe's era had for him. I wanted my teammates to like me and I believe they did. I don't think that mattered greatly to Joe. They held him in awe and tried to give him all the space they could. He was a custodian of the Yankee tradition. That was never my ambition, and I'm not sure it was Joe's, but it came naturally to him.

There was never any real tension or jealousy between us—we weren't that close. But it's hard to explain how much the players on the team liked to analyze him. I never tired of hearing the stories.

It's hard to capture the qualities he had. He was distant and austere, but a man of honor. He was unforgiving of conduct that he considered crude or cheap or below the belt. Hardly anyone would confront Joe about his own actions, but a salty old writer named Jimmy Cannon once did and he came away with a pretty fair insight.

In the '47 Series, the Dodgers's Jackie Robinson had gone out of the baseline to throw a rolling block into Phil Rizzuto, who was completing a double play. There was some booing and then the inning was over. Later in the game, DiMaggio ran out a routine ground ball and Robinson, who was playing first base and not very experienced at it, had his foot planted on the bag. It was almost an invitation to a spiking, but Joe twisted his body sideways as he crossed the base and avoided him.

After the game, Cannon asked him why he hadn't stepped on Jack's foot after what he had done to Rizzuto. DiMaggio considered the question for a moment and said, "I thought about it running down to first base, and then it occurred to me that Phil's an Italian, I'm an Italian, and Robinson is black. I didn't want anyone to think it was the guineas against the niggers. If Phil was black or Robinson an Italian, I guess I would have spiked him."

As Cannon noted, that was a lot of thinking for three and a half seconds of running, but DiMaggio had a kind of puritan instinct. When Charlie Dressen, who was a disciple of Durocher, joined the Yankees as a coach, he once protested an umpire's call by flinging towels and batting helmets out of the dugout.

He was in the midst of making this mess when DiMaggio suddenly appeared at his side. "Go out and pick up that stuff, now," said Joe, making it an order. Dressen started to say something and Joe cut him off. "Charlie," he said, "on this ballclub when we don't like decisions, we don't throw things. We hit home runs."

To me, DiMaggio's fifty-six-game hitting streak is the third most impressive of those that have been on the books for more than fifty years. Two others may be harder to break: Lou Gehrig's iron-man string and Johnny Vander Meer's back-to-back no-hitters in 1939. Gehrig did not miss a game for nearly fourteen seasons, a record so astonishing that you can't imagine anyone *watching* so many games, much less playing in them. A pitcher may one day equal the feat of Vander Meer, but the idea of anyone beating him—that is, pitching three consecutive no-hitters—is so unlikely, your home computer would probably laugh if you asked for the odds.

Yet no record in sports has the weight and aura of DiMaggio's streak. Part of this attraction is DiMaggio himself, a man so reserved he was almost a mystery. But I think what really grips us as fans is the link from one era to another. I broke in as Joe was leaving the stage. Ruth's last game was in 1935 and DiMaggio came up a year later. He extended his hitting streak to twenty-four games on the day Lou Gehrig died in June of 1941.

The numbers are there to be jiggled with and admired. They make it possible to place legends of different generations—Nolan Ryan and Walter Johnson, Henry Aaron and

Babe Ruth, Pete Rose and Ty Cobb—under the same microscope. The joy is in comparing the people and the changing times. When Rose hit safely in forty-four games in 1978, topping the National League mark and threatening to overtake DiMaggio, reporters almost had to punch him in the mouth to get him to stop talking.

As an individual, Pete was as different from Joe as Muhammad Ali was from Joe Louis. DiMaggio suppressed his emotions so much that he developed ulcers. During his streak, he smoked as many as three packs of cigarettes a day, ducking into the dugout runway between innings for a drag. He would have lit one in center field if they had let him.

He said he always expected the streak to be broken, but he was amused by the excuses that were given to explain why no one has. One of the arguments is that travel in the jet age is more hectic and more draining. Joe didn't buy that one, and neither do I. "Train travel wasn't easy," he said. "We would leave New York after a game, ride twenty-four hours to St. Louis and sometimes go right from the station to the ballpark for a night game. The guys batting third, fourth, and fifth got a break with the berths. We would get the ones in the middle of the car. The rookies and utility players had to sleep over the wheels."

The Yankees were already a dynasty when Stengel took over as manager, and I think DiMaggio was the only player who ever made Casey nervous. Bone spurs in his feet troubled Joe his last two or three seasons, and while he frequently played hurt, he didn't like the idea of people seeing him at less than his best.

Once, the reporters went to Casey in the clubhouse and asked him for that day's lineup. "I can't give you the lineup yet," he said, glancing at DiMaggio, who was bent over tying his shoes. Joe said nothing and Casey kept jabbering with the writers, his eyes still stuck on DiMaggio. Finally, Joe straightened up and with just the slightest motion nodded his head. "Now I can give you the lineup," Stengel said. Joe had confirmed that he would be able to play.

I learned a few things about fame over the years, but DiMaggio was a different kind of famous. I can't picture strangers coming up to him, as they did to me, and putting their arms around his shoulder and spilling beer in his lap. It is hard to be really honest with yourself when you try to remember how you felt forty years ago. But I admired him then and still do. There was nothing not to like about Joe; he wouldn't let just anybody get close to him, and after a certain time in my career I understood that.

He was beyond question one of the great players of the century. Then he became something more, when Paul Simon and Art Garfunkel wrote a song called "Mrs. Robinson" for the movie *The Graduate*, and it had a line that sent the country on a mass-identity crisis: "Where have you gone, Joe DiMaggio, a nation turns its lonely eyes to you . . ."

That lyric became a commentary on sports and its role in society and in our fantasy lives. I read where Paul Simon, a lifelong Yankee fan, tried to explain what it meant. He said, "It has something to do with heroes. People who are all good with no bad in them. That's the way I always saw Joe DiMaggio."

# HERE'S TO YOU, MR. ROBINSON

## 1952—YANKEES 4, DODGERS 3

There was just nothing to match the rivalry and madness of facing the Brooklyn Dodgers in the World Series, as the Yankees would in 1952, and four of the next five years. These were the "Boys of Summer," although Roger Kahn wouldn't give them that perfect description until a couple decades later.

I look at the lineup today and think, what players, what talent, what fans they had! Duke Snider and Carl Furillo in the outfield; Gil Hodges, Jackie Robinson, Pee Wee Reese, and Billy Cox in the infield; Roy Campanella behind the plate. The pitchers included Joe Black, Carl Erskine, Billy Loes, and Preacher Roe.

It isn't easy to imagine a team more perfectly suited to

a place and time. And I thought how great the Yankees must have been to beat them every year but one. We were a fairly loose collection of individuals, and Casey Stengel knew how to run us through the blender. No one platooned players, moved them around, like Casey and not everybody liked it. But you couldn't argue with the results.

Coming from Oklahoma, it took me a few years to get used to the native language of Brooklyn. Erskine was pronounced "Oisken" by the Flatbush Faithful. They looked forward each October to the "Woild Serious." I found out later that the Dodger fans were the ones who gave the Waner brothers, Paul and Lloyd, their colorful nicknames. I thought Big Poison and Little Poison referred to their deadly skills at bat. Turns out that when they would walk to the plate for the Pittsburgh Pirates, the Dodger fans recognized them by their size: it was the way they said, here comes the big person (Paul), or here comes the little person (Lloyd). The nicknames stuck.

Also, there was something special about a Subway Series, a rivalry that has all but vanished from the scene. When I was a rookie, remember, you had three teams in New York and two each in Chicago, Boston, St. Louis, and Philadelphia.

Of course, we didn't take the subway. But the first day we boarded the team bus to take us to Ebbets Field, all the way out Second Avenue the fans were cheering and holding up signs of support. As soon as we crossed the bridge into Brooklyn, and turned onto Flatbush Avenue, it was like entering another world. The faces were flushed and contorted, the fans were screaming and cursing at us. They weren't too happy with us the last two games of the '52 Series either, especially the twenty-year-old kid batting third and playing center field.

All of which reminded me how far we had to come—Casey, the team, and me—from the doubts and distractions of Florida in the early spring. The Yankees trained that year in St. Petersburg, and the big story in camp was who would replace DiMaggio in center field.

It had been understood, or hoped, that I would, because as young as I was that meant the job would be filled for a lot of years to come. The problem was that my knee hadn't fully healed, it wasn't stable, and I came to camp still hobbling around. No one blamed me for being hurt, but I knew how little I had done in the off-season to rehabilitate the knee and I was carrying some guilt.

I didn't have anywhere near my full speed and I couldn't make the cuts, the sudden starts and stops. Casey knew I wasn't ready to replace DiMaggio, but I competed for the job with Bob Cerv and Jackie Jensen in the spring. When we broke camp to open the season, I was installed in right field, where I'd be putting less strain on my leg.

Cerv didn't have the speed for center and Jensen was a right-handed hitter who was cheated by the dimensions of Yankee Stadium. The Yankees showed their concern in early May by trading Jensen and pitcher Spec Shea to Washington for Irv Noren, a veteran center fielder. I couldn't believe they had given up on Jensen so quickly, but Casey was quoted as saying that the trade would give him a chance to find out if he could play. He found out, all right. In 1954 the Senators sent him to Boston and Jackie went on to lead the league in runs batted in three times. He won the Most Valuable Player award in 1958.

My world was changing awfully fast, or so it seemed. I was still so country and so naive that the Yankees had to get me out of a deal I had signed with an agent, giving him 50 percent of my contract for the next ten years.

And I was a married man now. The year before, I had roomed with Hank Bauer and Johnny Hopp in the apartments over the Stage Delicatessen, and I had gained twenty-five pounds on a fairly steady diet of matzoh ball soup and corned beef sandwiches.

While I had traveled north with the team, Merlyn

packed up the car and drove alone from Commerce to New York. We had a room that summer at the Concourse Plaza Hotel, a tiny bathroom, a bed, a chair, bare walls, no stove or refrigerator, and no TV set—at $10 a month we couldn't afford to rent one.

When the club went on the road, Merlyn was alone for up to two weeks. It couldn't have been easy for her, but she never complained. I would leave her $20 or so for food and spending money, and tell her if she ran short to charge it to the room. She never did. She spent most of the time visiting the other players' wives, and if they had kids she'd fill up on cookies.

And we still needed jobs in the winter to get by. Merlyn worked as a filing clerk at the bank in Commerce. I didn't have to go down into the mines anymore, but I had a job waiting for me with a construction company owned by a friend, Harold Youngman.

On May 6, three days after the Jensen trade, as I was dressing to go to the ballpark, Casey called the hotel. He told me my mother had tried to reach me at the ballpark. Instead, Casey gave me the message: My father had died.

Even though I had watched his health decline, the news hit me hard. He had spent his final months at the hospital in Denver, the final selfless act in a life of unselfishness.

I went home to Commerce for the funeral. I thought about how much it meant to my dad for me to make it in baseball, to avoid the grim and empty life he had known breaking rocks in the zinc mines. He had planned my future for me, although I think it was just a coincidence that I was born during the World Series of 1931. That was the one where Pepper Martin and the Cardinals ran wild on Mickey Cochrane. But that didn't stop my dad from naming me after the Detroit catcher out of loyalty.

From the time I started showing promise, my Christmas present each year was a new baseball glove. It may be hard to believe the multimillion-dollar salaries that are paid to today's players. But when I think back, almost as unbelievable to me is the memory of Mutt Mantle spending $22, most of his paycheck, on the best glove he could find, a Marty Marion model.

I rejoined the Yankees after missing five games. I don't want to put too fine a point on this, or make it some kind of hearts-and-flowers deal. But from then on I was a different ballplayer. Before I left the club I was batting over .300, but not running well or hitting for much power.

On May 20, I made my first start of the season in center field and had four hits. Stengel was watching me, testing me. I played a couple more games, moved back to right field, went to the bench, then returned to center on June 3. I had four more hits. Somewhere in that stretch I even played a game at third base. I had four chances and made two errors, for a .500 fielding average.

Bobby Brown was a part-time starter at third, and I think he was joking when he said, after the game, "That's it. I'm going to retire." But a few years later he did, went to medical school, became a doctor, and eventually returned to baseball as president of the American League. I don't want to take credit for all that, but Bobby must have seen something in the way I played third base that persuaded him to take life more seriously.

On June 15, in Cleveland's Municipal Stadium, the Yankees swept a doubleheader. I had just one hit in nine at bats, but it was a three-run homer, my fourth of the season and my first from the left side of the plate. But the game was significant for another reason: I was in center field to stay. My knee had improved to the point that I could cover the ground. Casey had decided that I was ready to take on the legacy of Joe DiMaggio.

We were in a two-team race with the Indians the rest of the summer, and wrapped up the title on September 26 at Philadelphia's Shibe Park, beating the A's in eleven innings, 5-2. Irv Noren and I both had solo homers, I led off the top of the eleventh with a single, and Billy Martin drove in the last two runs.

The A's operated on a shoestring, but they had a great pitcher in the wispy left-hander Bobby Shantz, and a tough one in Harry Byrd. One of my regrets was getting to the majors a year after Connie Mack retired as manager, at eighty-eight. He was the only manager who couldn't be fired because he owned the team. I knew from the photographs what a grand sight he was, sitting in the dugout in his suit, starched collar, and straw hat, a thin and courtly looking man. He began his career in baseball as a catcher in 1883—he must have been around when they cleared a cow pasture and laid out the first diamond.

Jimmy Dykes replaced Mr. Mack, who passed over his two sons, Earle, one of his coaches, and Roy, who worked in the front office. The sons were in their sixties, but the players apparently didn't treat them with much respect. There was a story told about the time Earle Mack went to the mound to take Bobo Newsom, a rubber-armed, hard-headed pitcher, out of a game. "Daddy says you should leave now," Earle told him.

"Well, you can just tell Daddy," said Bobo, "to go screw hisself."

I finished the 1952 season hitting .311 with 23 homers, 87 runs batted in, 94 runs scored, and 111 strikeouts. That last figure led the league and set a new club record. That was the one conflict my stubbornness never allowed me to cure. I hated striking out, but I always tried to kill the ball. I always said that I was as strong as Ted Williams and Stan Musial, but they were content to meet the ball. I wanted to make it explode. Stengel worked on me for years to cut down on my swing, and we had some heated arguments. When Casey was ticked off, he didn't talk in circles, you could understand him real plain. He finally gave up trying to change me, and we didn't argue nearly as much.

Stengel joined John McGraw of the Giants and Joe McCarthy, who had assembled the previous Yankee dynasty, as the only managers to win four pennants in a row. Of course, the '52 Yankees had not been favored to repeat. Not only was DiMaggio gone, with his quiet leadership and all the symbolism, but Ed Lopat had a sore arm, Bobby Brown and Jerry Coleman had military obligations, and Billy Martin cracked his ankle during spring training.

Our pitching staff was getting long in the tooth, with Allie Reynolds, Vic Raschi, Johnny Sain, and Lopat as the starters. But they were accustomed to winning, and so were Rizzuto, Berra, Bauer, and Collins. I was part of the new blood. Billy Martin made the team in the spring of 1950 and Whitey Ford was called up in June, but after the season left to serve two years in the army. Gil McDougald and I came up the next year, and we would have to wait until 1953 before the new gang was all here.

The Yankees always seemed to have players coming and going, bringing up two or three rookies, making a late season deal for a veteran, a Johnny Mize or Johnny Hopp or Enos Slaughter. The Dodgers, by contrast, seemed to have an almost permanent cast.

Snider arrived in 1947, so he was established when Willie Mays and I made it to New York. Duke and I were both labeled temper cases in our early years, and between us we kicked a lot of water coolers and dented a few dugout walls. He was also accused of not getting the most out of his ability, but he tied Ralph Kiner's National League record for hitting forty or more home runs in five straight seasons. He also criticized the fans in Brooklyn for booing him, and so they booed all the more. From what I knew of the Dodger fans, that might not have been real smart.

It was said that Branch Rickey brought up Snider in '47, and hailed him as the successor to Pete Reiser in center field, at least partly in the hope of diverting some of the commotion that was guaranteed to surround Jackie Robinson. If that was the strategy, it failed. The recognition Duke deserved as a complete player didn't come quickly. For one thing, he was on a team that had more than its share of larger-than-life players. Then he ran into the same ceiling I did, the sense that no matter how well you did you could have done better.

I was in high school when Jackie Robinson broke the color line, so the full drama of that time didn't really register on me. Still, the Yankees were one of the last teams in baseball with an all-white roster, and it wouldn't be integrated until 1956, when Elston Howard arrived. This didn't go unnoticed, but there was no explanation that I ever heard. I don't think Del Webb and Dan Topping, who owned the club, or George Weiss, the general manager, were bigots. But the Yankees were winning, and Casey felt no pressure to seek out the gifted players who were available, as the Negro Leagues, once the only option for such heroic names as Satchel Paige and Josh Gibson, faded away.

The 1952 World Series opened at Ebbets Field and, as great as they were, the Dodgers still had a quality of daffiness that dated back to leaner, losing times. You didn't know whether to feel sorry for the Dodgers or to view them as you would a dangerous, wounded animal. The team had blown the pennant on the last day of the two previous seasons. An article had appeared in a national magazine under the byline of Charlie Dressen, the Dodgers' manager, entitled "It Won't Happen Again." Asked if he wasn't taking a risk, Dressen replied that he had been paid $3,000 and there was no risk at all. "If we lose this year," he said, "I'll be fired anyway."

A day or so before the Series began, a reporter polled a number of the players on both teams for their predictions. When the story appeared the next day, one of the Dodgers, Billy Loes, was quoted as saying he thought the Yankees would win in seven games. Dressen was nearly choking with disbelief when he confronted his pitcher. Loes replied that he had been misquoted. "I picked 'em in six," he said.

Dressen had a mild surprise for us. His starter in the opener was Joe Black, a big rookie who had appeared in relief in fifty-four games during the season, and won fifteen, but had started only twice. Black went the distance to beat us, 4-2, and while the Dodgers had only six hits off Allie Reynolds, half of them were homers by Robinson, Snider, and Reese.

Vic Raschi, always a money pitcher, got us even in Game 2, winning 7-1 on a three-hitter. We broke the game open with five runs in the sixth, as Billy Martin tagged Loes—who had relieved Carl Erskine—for a three-run homer into the seats in left. I had two singles and a double, but it kind of bugged me that Billy hit a World Series homer before I did.

The Series moved to Yankee Stadium and the third game matched two crafty old-timers, both thirty-four and both left-handed, our Eddie Lopat and the Dodgers' Preacher Roe. At the All-Star Game in 1951, Lopat told Roe to watch closely when Stan Musial came to bat because he had figured out a way to pitch to him. Musial faced Eddie in the fourth inning and lined his first offering into the right-field seats. From across the field, Preacher shouted to him, "I see what you mean, but I found that way to pitch to him a long time ago, all by myself."

Johnny Mize hit a pinch homer off Roe in the ninth, but it wasn't enough as the Dodgers won, 5-3, to take a two games to one lead. Berra also homered, but he was miserable in the clubhouse because Reese and Robinson worked a double steal in the top of the ninth, and both scored on a pitch that got past Berra for a passed ball. Tom Gorman had come on in relief, and he threw a low fastball that glanced off Yogi's hand, split his finger, and rolled to the backstop. Both pitchers were suspected of throwing spitters, but Gorman's pitch just got away, and the two runs were the difference.

The loss was the first ever for Lopat in the World Series. For the second time in three days, we trailed the Dodgers. We were now at that stage where you could practically see the gears grinding in the minds of the managers. For Game 4, both brought their starters back on two days' rest, and this time Reynolds threw a four-hit shutout to beat Joe Black,

2-0. Reynolds, known as the Chief, struck out ten, fanning Jackie Robinson three times.

We were even again, at least for a day. Having made only a cameo appearance before getting hurt in '51, I was now fully conscious of the joys of being twenty and playing in the only show in town. I felt how the tension clawed at you and drove teams to take bigger gambles. I became more aware of the inside game, the part the fans missed, and how it controlled the action.

The Dodgers were only down by a run when they tried to score Andy Pafko from third on a suicide squeeze. If the play worked, we had a new game. Dressen was his own third-base coach, and he went through all the nervous fiddling, rubbing his hands, pulling at the bill of his cap, slapping his thigh, kicking the dust, hitching at his belt. For only a moment, he put one hand to his throat.

At that precise instant, Allie Reynolds spun around and let the pitch go, a fastball too low and outside for the batter to bunt. The ball plunked into Berra's glove and he turned to meet Pafko, who was still ten feet from home and a dead duck.

Dressen had overlooked one thing, and that one thing was standing at second base—Billy Martin. He had played for Charlie at Oakland in the Pacific Coast League, and as soon as Dressen went to his throat he knew they were going to squeeze. It was the same sign they had used at Oakland. He signaled Berra, who passed it along to Reynolds.

A stolen sign had killed a Dodger rally.

Snider was the hero the next day, with a single to tie the score and a double in the eleventh inning to win it, 6-5. Brooklyn now led, three games to two, with the Series going back to Ebbets Field, meaning that we had to win twice at their park.

The matchup for Game 6 was Vic Raschi against Billy Loes, the brash young right-hander from Queens. Snider's solo homer in the sixth produced the game's first run. In the seventh, we scored twice to go ahead. Berra homered for the first run, and the second scored when Raschi bounced a single off the leg of Loes, who said later that he "lost the ball in the sun."

The runner, Gene Woodling, had moved into scoring position when Loes balked, the ball squirting out of his hand like a melon seed. After the game, he explained that one by saying, "Too much spit."

I led off the eighth, batting left-handed, and connected for my first World Series homer, into the bleachers in left-center. As it turned out, we needed that run because Snider continued to make a nuisance of himself, hitting his second homer of the game in the eighth with the bases empty. Reynolds, who seemed to be on twenty-four-hour call, came in from the bull pen to retire the last four batters and protect the win, 3-2. The Series was now down to one game.

In the clubhouse, Loes told reporters that the ball I hit was on the inside and I was falling away from it when I swung. "Where would he have put it if he had really been taking his cut?" asked Billy, answering his own question. "It would have gone over the roof—or something."

There isn't anything in sports quite like the seventh game of a World Series. Unlike the Super Bowl, it has taken you a week of games, not interviews, to get there. You roll out of bed and start over every day. You play offense and defense.

The importance of the pitching is magnified by the pressures of the Series. A staff may be ten deep during the season, but the managers either play hunches or go to the guys who have been the most reliable. Casey decided to go with Eddie Lopat, and Dressen put his hopes on Joe Black, making his third start.

The game was tied at 2-2 in the sixth inning when I stepped to the plate with one out and the bases empty. Black threw me a slider, I think, and I got all of it. The ball soared high and deep, over the scoreboard in right field and landing on the other side of Bedford Avenue. Eyeball measurements spotted the homer at 450 feet. I never put much faith in those figures; it's like getting a wrecker driver to estimate the damage to your car. But the fans seemed to be impressed with them and I guess they didn't do any harm.

The homer was my second in two games, and I knew this one might decide the game and the Series. I tried not to show how excited I was. I kept my head down, but I think that was the fastest I ever ran around the bases. An inning later, I singled in the final run.

Reynolds, Raschi, and Bob Kuzava followed Lopat to the mound. Kuzava was a stringy left-hander, who had pitched for the White Sox and Senators before joining the Yankees in a trade. He was what the press called a journeyman, who would pitch for five more teams before his ten-year career came to an end. But he was a classic example of a lesser-known guy who had his moment of glory in the World Series.

Kuzava entered the game with one out in the seventh, the bases loaded, Duke Snider at bat, and Jackie Robinson in the on-deck circle. He got Snider on an infield pop and then went to a 3 and 2 count on Robinson. Jackie lifted a pop fly near the mound, and a swirling wind blew it away from Joe Collins, the first baseman, who was looking into the sun. The runners were all moving when my roomie, Billy Martin, made a sprinting, lunging catch to save the lead and probably the game.

The score was still 4-2 and it ended that way as Kuzava throttled the Dodgers the last two innings. The Yankees had run their World Series winning streak to four, and I knew I had been a factor in this one. I was still thirteen days shy of my twenty-first birthday and my heart was almost orbiting the earth.

A really extraordinary thing happened in that Series. Gil Hodges, the Dodger first baseman, went 0 for 21 and the Brooklyn fans *never booed him.* It was agonizing to watch. He walked five times and struck out six and scored one run, but no matter how hard he tried that first hit wouldn't come. But the fans treated him gently because he was, first of all, a nice man with that quiet strength, like a forest, where the lack of noise isn't the same as a lack of life.

He was a midwesterner, but he made his home in Brooklyn and the fans forgave him his failure and kept pulling for him. In the seventh game, he flied out, lined out, hit into a double play and was safe on an error, and the fans applauded each time he came to bat. Over the years, I knew how fans reacted when I was in a slump, or Snider, or most other players, and this was something to see.

After the game, Jackie Robinson came into our clubhouse and shook my hand. He said, "You're a helluva ballplayer and you've got a great future." I thought that was a classy gesture, one I wasn't then capable of making. I was a bad loser. What meant even more was what Jackie told the press: "Mantle beat us. He was the difference between the two teams. They didn't miss DiMaggio."

I have to admit, I became a Jackie Robinson fan on the spot. And when I think of that World Series, his gesture is what comes to mind. Here was a player who had without doubt suffered more abuse and more taunts and more hatred than any player in the history of the game. And he had made a special effort to compliment and encourage a young white kid from Oklahoma.

I made it a point to learn a little more about Jackie. When the Dodgers signed him to a minor league contract in 1946, there were no black generals or senators or Supreme Court justices, and no black children in white southern schools. His arrival in Brooklyn was a turning point for baseball and probably for the country.

The story needs no retelling about how Branch Rickey decided to break the color barrier, how he chose Robinson, and how he signed him with one condition—he could not react to openly racist attacks. The Jackie Robinson I knew was wound tight and combative, but he held his temper. After he established himself as a superb hitter, fielder, and base runner, he was no longer reluctant to express his anger. By then he had won the loyalty of his teammates and the respect of all but the most die-hard of his opponents.

His first manager, Leo Durocher, helped convince the Dodgers to accept him by pointing out, "He can put a lot of money in your pockets." Leo meant by helping them win championships, and that he did.

On the day of his first game in the major leagues, in 1947, Robinson stood alone in the Dodger infield while Gladys Gooding sang the "Star-Spangled Banner" and then the Brooklyn pitcher, Joe Hatten, took his warm-ups. During those minutes, out of the dugout of the visiting Boston Braves poured a steady stream of racial insults, and then a dramatic thing happened. Pee Wee Reese, a southerner from Kentucky and the captain of the Dodgers, walked over to Jackie and stood beside him. And the insults stopped.

Robinson never let anyone, not his teammates and not his opponents, forget that he was a man. All he expected was to be treated like one. Based on what he achieved, that didn't seem too much to ask.

We had one other shared moment in the World Series. He lined a single to right-center and the ball skipped into my glove on three hops. He rounded first base, acting as if he would stop. I used to pick guys off first on that play pretty often. This time Casey had warned me Robinson would be watching for my throw. So after I fielded the ball on the bounce, I faked a throw behind him. Sure enough, he took off for second base. I threw to Billy and we had him out.

I'll never forget the sight: Jackie getting up, dusting himself off, and giving me a little tip of the hat, his eyes saying, "I'll get you next time."

# THE DYNASTY CONTINUES

## 1953—YANKEES 4, DODGERS 2

There was a time when the host of a radio show could ask a guest in the audience where he or she was from, and if they said, "Brooklyn," everybody laughed or applauded. I don't know why. They just did. Those days are gone. So are the Dodgers and that may be the connection.

It seemed to take a special kind of person to live there, hardy and proud and almost indifferent to the world around them. It was a little like living in Tibet. They had what we would later call fatal instincts. These are my two classic Brooklyn Dodger stories, one I saw and one I heard about.

In one of the World Series games, a close call went against the Dodgers, and a fan leaped out of the stands and jumped on the back of George Magerkurth, the plate umpire, who weighed three hundred pounds and had been an amateur boxer in his youth. The photograph ran in a lot of papers, showing this guy in his early twenties, sitting on

George's chest and flailing at him with his fists until the cops and ushers pulled him off.

It turned out the fan was on parole for petty theft, but Magerkurth refused to press charges, explaining, "I have a boy of my own." A few years later, the same fellow was arrested and tried as a pickpocket, and he appeared before a Judge Leibovitz, who was a Dodger fan and had been at the game the day of the fight with big George. He kept looking at him, trying to place him, and finally he said: "I've seen you someplace. Ebbets Field?"

"That's right," said the defendant, proudly. "Ebbets Field."

The judge gave him a sentence of five to ten years, but added, "They play ball up there on Sundays. You won't find it so bad." Then he asked him, as a fan, "How did you come to lose your head that day . . . especially with a big one like Magerkurth?"

And the guy laughed, pleased that the judge remembered his great day. "I was pretty stirred up," he said. "The Dodgers shoulda won that game easy. But just between you and me, judge, I had a partner in the stands that day. We were doing a little business." The guy was creating a disturbance so his partner could get into some pockets.

When Leo Durocher managed the Dodgers, a fan named Hilda Chester gained a following of her own. She had lungs of leather and carried a cowbell to all the home games and rang it with real energy. During one game, she called out to Pete Reiser, the center fielder, and from her seat in the stands tossed a wadded-up piece of paper onto the field. "Give it to Leo," she yelled. At the end of the inning, Reiser stopped on his way to the bench to say hello to Larry MacPhail, the general manager whose box seat was next to the dugout. Then he gave the note to Durocher.

The next inning, after Whitlow Wyatt gave up a long out and a single, Leo brought in Hugh Casey from the bull pen. Casey was hit hard and almost blew a big Dodger lead.

After the game, an angry Durocher confronted Reiser,

"Don't you *ever* give me another note from MacPhail as long as you play for me."

The surprised Reiser said, "That note was from Hilda."

"From *Hilda*?" screamed Leo. "You mean to say that wasn't from MacPhail?" The note, which Reiser hadn't read, said, "Get Casey hot. Wyatt's losing it." Leo had let a fan with a cowbell tell him when to change pitchers.

But this was October 1953, and the Dodgers had slowly outgrown the image of their daffier days. They had won the National League pennant that season by thirteen games over the Milwaukee Braves, who had moved out of Boston and into America's dairyland. That was the year's big story in baseball.

The story didn't have any great meaning to the Yankees. To us it just meant the Red Sox had run the Braves out of town. No one I knew could imagine that the move would open the way for the Giants and Dodgers to abandon New York, leading to an era of expansion in baseball and new leagues in football, basketball, and ice hockey, with television as the sugar daddy.

The Yankees had won the pennant for the fifth straight year, a record, and were trying to match that streak in the Series. A lot of people were already tired of us winning all the time. On the day of the opening game, President Eisenhower and former President Truman both told reporters they hoped we would lose.

That may have been the only issue they agreed on. Truman was quoted as saying, "The Yankees are getting to be a habit. It's time somebody did something about it."

I'm sure that feeling was shared by the Dodgers, who appeared to have the club to do it. Carl Furillo had won the National League batting title with an average of .344. Duke Snider had the first of his five straight seasons of hitting 40 or more home runs. Roy Campanella hit .312, with 41 homers, led the league in runs batted in with 142, and won the Most Valuable Player award for the second time in three years.

Jackie Robinson hit .329 and Gil Hodges .302, with 31 homers. Snider, Campanella, Hodges, Robinson, Pee Wee Reese, and Junior Gilliam all scored more than 100 runs. Their numbers would bend the back of a camel. They fed you all those stats and then said their strength was the pitching staff. Carl Erskine had 20 wins, and Russ Meyer, Billy Loes, Preacher Roe, and their relief ace, Clem Labine, all won in double figures.

That team was actually the one Roger Kahn wrote about in *Boys of Summer*. He was then in his early twenties, in his second and last season covering the Dodgers for the *New York Herald-Tribune*. Duke told me years later that most of the players felt that Roger overplayed the angle of hard adjustments and sad times in the real world. But the book tapped into the sentimental grip that baseball has on people, including the players, and captured the special character of that Dodger team. The book didn't make them famous, though. Their bats and gloves did that.

The Dodgers had run away with their race and we did the same, finishing eight games in front of Cleveland. I had pulled a muscle in my left thigh and reinjured my knee in August, and again I wouldn't be at full speed for the Series. That was when the trainer, Gus Mauch, started wrapping my legs like a mummy's, from the ankle all the way up to the hip. Casey stayed on my back pretty hard for getting hurt. It was as if he blamed the injuries on my temper or my lack of concentration. "You tell the fresh kid something," he said, referring to Billy, "and he listens and does it. You tell the other fellow something and he acts like you tell him nothing."

Casey wanted me to shorten my swing so I wouldn't strike out so much. I think the old man expected so much from me, he wouldn't accept the idea that what I did was nearly all instinct. I had almost no grasp of the technical or tactical sides of the game. I just didn't want to mess up my stroke, and I didn't say much because I was afraid I'd say something dumb.

I was going to have a Series of highs and lows, and I was starting to wonder if that would be the pattern of my whole career, feast or famine. I had the feeling I was on the end of a yo-yo string. They were either measuring my homers or adding up my strikeouts.

My cheering section had grown by one, sort of. Our first son had been born in April, and I learned about it during an exhibition game in Brooklyn. When I came to bat, the public address announcer said, "Mickey doesn't know it yet, but he just became the father of an eight-pound, twelve-ounce baby boy."

We named him Mickey Elvin, the middle name after my dad, but from the start everyone called him Mickey Jr. I rented our first house that summer of 1953 in New Jersey, and in July I went out to the airport and picked up Merlyn and little Mick. It wasn't an easy summer. The baby was sick with asthma and had an allergy to milk.

But he was the redheaded grandson my father had wanted. More than ever, I wished I had been able to tell him how much I loved him. I don't mean at the hospital. I mean ever. I never did. The Mantles just didn't express those feelings and I can't explain why. I've never told my sons that I love them. But they know I do.

The pressure on me had grown. Here I was, twenty-two, with a wife and baby to support and a widowed mother back home. More than ever, I needed to prove that I belonged in Yankee pinstripes.

Even before the opener, Merlyn had a good Series. On Thursday, she was on a network television show and they gave her $1,000 worth of merchandise. I'm not sure anything I did in the days to come thrilled her more.

No matter what was happening on the edges, who we played or how I felt, the atmosphere before the first game was always special to me. This was the fiftieth anniversary of the first World Series ever held, between the 1903 Boston and Pittsburgh teams. Cy Young, who is considered the greatest pitcher who ever lived, threw out the first ball. The award given out every year to the best pitcher in each league carries his name. I guess he was in his mid- to late seventies. He stood on the mound, a little stiffly, and lobbed one to Yogi, who delivered the ball to Commissioner Ford Frick's box for safekeeping. Frick was sitting with Grantland Rice, the sportswriter who gave Notre Dame's "Four Horsemen" their name.

Rice smiled as ol' Cy Young returned to his seat. "That," he said, "was not the delivery I knew in 1903."

I don't care how cool a ballplayer tries to act. I've never known one who wasn't impressed to be in the same ballpark as a Ty Cobb or a Cy Young. It's like watching statues come to life. But you don't have much time to gawk. There is always a sudden flurry of activity on the benches that tells you the game is about to begin. Everybody's nervous. The Dodgers were late turning in their lineup card because Charlie Dressen couldn't find his lucky pencil stub.

Casey wasn't worried about any good luck charms. He was worried about Allie Reynolds. We needed a win out of Reynolds in the opener to line up our starting rotation. The Chief was fine while he lasted, but he didn't last through the sixth. He gave up a leadoff homer to Hodges and a two-run, pinch-hit homer to George Shuba and Johnny Sain came in to get the win.

For the Dodgers, Carl Erskine couldn't get through the first inning. He walked the first three batters and we scored four runs, three on a bases-loaded triple by Billy Martin. In the bottom of the seventh, Joe Collins broke a 5-5 tie with a two-out homer and we finished them off, 9-5.

In a game that had twenty-four hits, five homers, two triples, and three doubles, it may sound odd to say that we won because we had the stronger arm. We did though. The arm was Yogi's and he made two terrific plays after the Dodgers had tied the score in the seventh and had two on with nobody out. First, Cox bunted and Berra barreled across the plate, pounced on the ball and threw to third to McDougald for a force play on Hodges. Now there was one out, with runners still at first and second. The Dodgers tried again to advance them. Clem Labine bunted. This time Yogi got to the ball even faster, and his throw beat Furillo cleanly at third. Then it was up to Junior Gilliam, who had a homer and a single. He fouled out—to Berra—to retire the side.

One of the benefits of being a center fielder is having those plays in front of you. I could see the entire action unfold. I'm not sure that the fans really appreciated how nimble Berra was. He was the best bad-ball hitter who ever lived and his exploits at bat probably kept him from getting all the credit he deserved behind the plate. Twice in his career I saw him grab a squeeze bunt, tag the batter before he could get out of the box, then dive to double the runner trying to score from third.

There was no doubt in my mind that the two best catchers in the game were on display when the Yankees and the Dodgers met in the 1950s. Campanella played the rest of the Series with a swollen hand; he was hit by a Reynolds pitch his first at bat. Campy was making up for lost time. He was twenty-seven when he reached the major leagues, the year after Robinson broke the color line. He would follow Jackie into the Hall of Fame in 1969.

Game 2 was one of those old-time pitching duels, a matchup between Eddie Lopat and Preacher Roe, who were in that category of veteran left-handers known as "junk men." This meant they threw with their brains as much as their arms. Lopat had a screwball, a slow curve, slider, change-up, and three knucklers.

Roe had an assortment just as soft, plus his spitter, which he said extended his career by seven years. Of course, he said this after he retired.

My shaky knee held up just fine when I went back to the wall in the third inning to run down Jackie Robinson's long drive with Pee Wee Reese on third and two out. The Dodgers had a 2-1 lead in the seventh, when Billy tied it with a home run that had just enough steam to reach the left-field seats, over the outstretched glove of Robinson.

Then it was my turn. In the bottom of the eighth, I stepped in with Hank Bauer on first and two away. The Preacher fell behind in the count, 2 and 0, and he surprised me with a change-up. It caught me slightly off stride, and I swung flat-footed, but I managed to hold the bat back just long enough to get my body into it. The ball settled into the seats in deep left field, and Jackie just looked up and kept his hands on his knees. The Dodgers outhit us, but Lopat stranded ten runners and we won, 4-2, to go up two games to none. We were feeling cocky as the Series moved to Ebbets Field.

Dressen had little choice but to bring back Erskine a day early to face Vic Raschi. Carl hadn't got out of the first inning in the opener, so he figured to be rested. Based on what we had seen so far, though, there wasn't any reason to think he would pitch a classic against us.

Both starters went the distance. In one of my most frustrating days, Erskine beat us, 3-2, striking out fourteen for a new World Series record. He fanned me four times and Joe Collins four times, using an overhand curve that would start out eye-high and then drop right in front of the plate. After one strikeout, I kicked the water cooler and Casey said, with that weariness in his voice, "Son, it ain't the water cooler striking you out."

On our bench, the veteran Johnny Mize was having a fit. "How can you guys keep swinging at that pitch in the dirt?" he demanded. He would finish his career with a lifetime average of .312 and 359 home runs, and he was headed for the Hall of Fame. He hated seeing guys chase bad pitches. I didn't say anything. After each strikeout I just carried my bat back to the bench and sat down, dazed.

To lead off the ninth inning, Casey sent up Don Bollweg to bat for Phil Rizzuto. This was where it helped to have a decent memory. Erskine had pitched against Bollweg in the minors, six or seven years earlier, and remembered that he had been a good low-ball hitter. So he threw him three fastballs, up and tight, and struck him out swinging. They announced over the public address system that Erskine had just tied the record for most strikeouts in a World Series at thirteen.

And here came Johnny Mize, batting for Raschi. Joe Collins and I leaned forward in our seats. After listening to Mize second-guess us all day, this was a confrontation we didn't want to miss. Carl started him off with a curve for a called strike. Then he came in with a fastball and Mize was a split-second late, fouling it back to the screen. Strike two. You could see Mize was agitated. That was his pitch, right down his wheelhouse. The next one was another one of those dive-bomber curves, and Mize swung weakly and missed. It tied him up so badly that he almost fell. He was strikeout number fourteen and he put himself in the record book.

When he sat down no one said a word.

There was one more moment of suspense left. Irv Noren batted for McDougald and walked, and that brought up Collins. Joe had hit the go-ahead homer in the first game, and the right-field fence in Ebbets Field was only 296 feet from home plate. Erskine knew that one bad pitch could cost him the game. You could almost hear his mind turning as he stood on the mound, motionless, waiting for Collins to get settled.

But his mind wasn't spinning any faster than Joe's. Talk about pressure. He did not want to become the first batter in fifty years of World Series history to strike out five times in a game. And even with what was at stake, and all the tension, a couple of the guys in our dugout were yelling at him, "Hey, Joe, this one's for the record."

Erskine came over the top with a curveball and Collins tapped a dribbler back to the mound. Erskine flipped it to Hodges to end the game. The winning run was scored on a home run by Campanella, sore hand and all, over the left-field wall in the bottom of the eighth.

Billy Loes, the pitcher who claimed he lost a ground

ball in the sun the previous October, and Duke Snider teamed up to beat us, 7-3, and even the series at two wins apiece. Duke blasted a homer and two doubles and drove in four runs.

And all that worrying Collins did the day before had been in vain. I struck out my first time up to make it five in a row, although not in one game.

We were suddenly looking puny. Hank Bauer overran Junior Gilliam's fly ball in the first inning, and it fell in for a double. When the inning ended, the Dodgers had three runs and our starter, Whitey Ford, was gone.

I was struggling so bad, I didn't know how things could get any worse, but I didn't have to wait long to find out. During batting practice, I stepped in front of the cage too soon and in self-defense I caught a line drive off the bat of Irv Noren with my bare hand. I was in pain. Stengel thought about taking me out of the lineup, but after Gus Mauch, our trainer, froze the hand with Xylocaine I insisted I could play.

I ought to explain about guys who play hurt. It wasn't some hairy-chested macho gesture. With the World Series, you had all winter to get well. And when players weren't knocking down a couple million dollars a year, the winner's share was worth a little pain. Part of it was fear; the fear that someone will think you took the easy way out; the fear of being replaced.

I'm glad I played because Game 5 turned out to be a slugfest and maybe the biggest game of my career, up to that point. And I had a chance to make up for my strikeouts. I came to the plate in the third inning, with the bases loaded. We had just broken a 1-1 tie with an unearned run and Charlie Dressen pulled his starter, the rookie left-hander, Johnny Podres. The relief pitcher was a right-hander, Russ Meyer, who was 15 and 5 that year, forcing me to turn around and bat lefty. World Series teams are thoroughly scouted. It was no secret to the Dodgers that my right knee sometimes buckled when I had to swing from the left side.

That was one reason Stengel kept urging me to punch the ball instead.

I jumped on Meyer's first pitch and sent a drive soaring to the opposite field, into the upper deck in left center, for a grand-slam home run. That put us ahead 6-1 and the Dodgers could never catch up. Casey dug past his aces and started Jim McDonald, who pitched into the eighth and got the win, 11-7. My name was added to a short list—Elmer Smith, 1920; Tony Lazzeri, 1936; and my teammate, Gil McDougald, 1951—as the only players to hit grand slams in the World Series.

This was Ebbets Field so the crowd wasn't exactly overjoyed. I had my head cocked so I could look into our dugout and for one of the few times in my career, I couldn't hold back a grin as I rounded the bases. At home plate, the guys who had scored ahead of me were waiting. They grabbed my hand, shoved me, slapped my back. The others came off the bench to maul me some more. They knocked my cap off and rubbed my crewcut and pulled me into the dugout.

They called Meyer the Mad Monk. I can't tell you why, but the nickname seemed to fit him. After the game, he said: "When you throw your best pitch and a guy hits it like that Mantle did, there's just nothing you can do about it. The pitch was a curveball, on the outside corner and just above Mickey's knees. Carl Erskine had told me that Mantle had been pulling away from almost every pitch. But on this one it was as if somebody had told him where the pitch was going to be. He stepped into it almost before I let the ball go."

More than thirty years later, Meyer said, almost proudly, "I believe it was the longest and hardest ball ever hit off me. I liked what Mickey said in an interview I read. He was asked what stands out in his mind as one of his big moments in baseball, and he replied that hitting the grand slam in the '53 Series off Russ Meyer 'who was a pretty fair country pitcher.' "

In those days that was a top-of-the-line compliment. It was like a saying we had in Oklahoma, "You might not believe in beauty contests, but if you entered one you want the judges to vote you purty."

The grand slam was a big moment in my life because baseball wasn't a game to me as the spectator understands it. It was my job and my living and all I knew. Without it, I was going to be digging fence posts back in Commerce or carrying a pick down to the zinc mines.

Now we went back to Yankee Stadium for the sixth game, and Dressen had to ask Erskine to give it another try on two days' rest. Whitey was on the mound for us. I'll say this, neither of them held anything back. Carl Furillo's two-run homer in the top of the ninth tied the score at 3-3. Then in the last of the ninth, with runners at first and second, Billy Martin lined a single through the infield. It was his twelfth hit of the Series and he scored Hank Bauer with the run that won the game, 4-3, and made the Yankees the World Champions for another year.

Personally, I had a strange Series. I batted only .208, going 5 for 24 and striking out eight times. But I won two games with homers and drove in seven runs, second only to Billy, with eight. Martin was carried off the field on the shoulders of his teammates. He always seemed to pump himself up for the Series. This time he batted an even .500. No one had ever before collected twelve hits in a six-game Series. It had been done twice in seven games, by Sam Rice of the Senators in 1925 and Pepper Martin of the Cardinals in 1931.

Stengel, at sixty-three, was now officially the most successful manager the game had known. He had won a record fifth straight World Series, passing John McGraw and Joe McCarthy. He lifted Whitey after seven innings and Allie Reynolds pitched the last two and picked up the win. In the clubhouse, Whitey said, "I felt bad when Casey took me out. Then I thought, well, he hasn't been wrong in five years."

Nine players had been with Stengel when the run started in 1949: Hank Bauer, Yogi Berra, Jerry Coleman, Joe Collins, Ed Lopat, Johnny Mize, Allie Reynolds, Phil Rizzuto, and Gene Woodling. I had played in the last three, but I wasn't anybody yet. I was still a prospect, or even a suspect.

It is impossible to write about 1953 and not clear up the story of the "tape-measure" home run, the phrase that sort of followed me around. The Yankees were in Griffith Stadium, in Washington, on the fourth day of the season; five days after the birth of my first son. There were two out in the fifth and Yogi had just drawn a walk when I came to bat against Chuck Stobbs, a lefty who started his career with the Red Sox. He pitched on some really feeble teams, and had to have a fine year just to win as many as he lost. He was 15 and 15 one season with the Senators, who usually finished last or close to it in that era.

I was hitting right-handed, using a bat I had borrowed from Loren Babe, an infielder who was with the Yankees only briefly.

Stobbs served up a fastball over the middle of the plate, just below the letters. I caught the ball on what hitters call the sweet spot on the bat. You always know when you do. The contact is so solid, so total, that there is no jarring, no recoil, no real sense of power. The bat just gives the ball a kiss, soft as a baby's breath.

This one left the playing field at the 391-foot mark in left-center, still climbing. It bounced off a beer sign on the football scoreboard 60 feet above the last row of bleachers. It sailed over Fifth Street and into the backyard of a two-story house at 434 Oakdale Street. Now this is what I was told: In the press box, Red Patterson, the Yankees' publicity director, jumped up from his seat and shouted, "That one has got to be measured." He bolted out of the press box and started looking for the spot where the ball landed. Red had been a top sportswriter for the *New York Herald-Tribune* some years earlier, and he still had a nose for a story.

Outside the ballpark, Red found a ten-year-old named Donald Dunaway who was holding the ball. The boy showed him where he found it and Red made a deal for the ball, trading a new ball, a glove, and some cash. The ball was lopsided and the cover was all scuffed up from hitting the beer sign and scraping the pavement.

Of course, Patterson didn't actually have a tape measure with him. He paced off the distance from the spot where it landed to the outside bleacher wall, and came up with 105 feet. Then he added the distance from home plate (391 feet) and 69 feet more from the fence to the rear wall of the bleachers. And when he got back to the press box he announced that the ball had traveled 565 feet.

It was the first ball ever to clear the left-field bleachers in Griffith Stadium, and there was something about the phrase—tape-measure home run—that stirred the fans and the press. It was talked about for weeks. The papers ran charts and graphs and diagrams, as if trying to show how the earth orbits the moon.

There was fairly brisk wind blowing that day and several writers pointed it out. Clark Griffith, the owner of the Senators, who was eighty-three and had been a player at the turn of the century, told the *Washington Star:* "Wind or no wind, nobody ever hit a ball that hard before."

At the end of the season, the ball was sent to the Hall of Fame along with Loren Babe's bat. The Senators raised a huge metal replica of a baseball to mark the spot where the ball grazed the beer sign. Bucky Harris, the manager, got tired of staring at it every day and had the baseball painted out.

I hit a total of twenty-nine homers in Griffith Stadium, but this was my first. It was a rough park for right-handed power hitters. There were 32 rows of seats in the left-field bleachers, and no ball had ever cleared them on the fly. And some right-handed hitters with awesome strength, Jimmie Foxx, Harmon Killebrew, and Josh Gibson, the great star of the Negro Leagues, all played there. In the season of 1945, the last of the war years, the entire Washington team hit only one home run at home and that was an inside-the-park job by Joe Kuhel.

No one ever pretended that the measurement was exact, and Red Patterson never went out and bought a tape measure. But this is what I have never before revealed. Years later, after he had moved to California and gone to work for the Dodgers, Red told me he never left the park. He was a hefty Irishman with a pink, flushed face, and exercise wasn't one of his strong points. By the time he walked down to the field level he was tired, so he stopped at a concession stand and had a couple of beers. I think the kid just showed up at the clubhouse wanting to sell the ball or get an autograph. After a while, Red made his way back to the press box and made his announcement.

After that, darned near every long homer had to have an estimated distance. By the end of the season, I had hit what was believed to be the longest home runs in Pittsburgh (in a preseason game), Washington, St. Louis, Detroit, Philadelphia, and Yankee Stadium.

The homer I hit in late September in Yankee Stadium off Billy Hoeft of Detroit carried 425 feet and smashed against a seat high in the upper deck in left field, 80 feet above ground level. The fans sitting in that section said the ball was still climbing, but I have learned that when people say such things their emotions may be talking.

Anyway, a professor of atmospheric research in Arizona concluded that the ball was probably moving at 155 miles an hour and would have traveled 620 feet if the stands hadn't got in the way. I don't honestly know what atmospheric research has to do with baseball. And I can't explain how you can tell from Arizona how far a ball hit in New York might have gone.

It is kind of crazy to argue about such things, but I have to admit that I enjoyed it. In our dugout that day, the players were listening to Bill Dickey, one of our coaches and a teammate of Ruth's. He was saying that Ruth and Foxx both hit balls farther than I did. After I hit the one that almost left the park, Jim McDonald, who was the winning pitcher in the game, asked innocently, "What did you just say, Bill?"

Dickey just rolled his eyes. "Forget what I said," he replied. "I've never seen a ball hit that hard."

I don't want that to come off as bragging, but I guess it does. The thing is, at the end of the season my numbers were not as good as they had been in '52. In June I was a contender for the triple crown, and made the All-Star Game for the first time, but then I hurt my thigh and re-injured the knee. I finished at .295, with twenty-one homers and ninety-two runs batted in.

So many wonderful things happened to me because of baseball, I really don't second-guess myself a lot. But I wish I had chopped up a few of those tape-measure homers and turned them into singles. In my own mind, that was the way I played, that was what I got paid to do, and I didn't give enough thought to hitting for average. I ended my career at .298 and it really bugs me not to be able to say that I was a .300 hitter.

# NEXT YEAR IS HERE

## 1955—DODGERS 4, YANKEES 3

I should have guessed that the 1955 season would have a tricky ending for us. It was the year *Damn Yankees* became one of the big hit musicals on Broadway, the saga of a baseball fan who sold his soul to the devil. It was based on a book called *The Year the Yankees Lost the Pennant*.

We had done that in 1954, and so had the Dodgers. I found out for the first time what it was like to miss the World Series. We won 103 games and finished 8 back of the Cleveland Indians. I would have thought that was impossible.

The Indians rolled to 111 wins behind one of the great pitching staffs of all time: Bob Feller, Bob Lemon, Early Wynn, and Mike Garcia. Then they lost four straight to Leo Durocher's Giants. That's baseball.

I suppose it's human nature, but the Yankees of my era looked on the World Series as a kind of birthright. The front office encouraged you to think of your player's shares as part of your salary. In those days you had to put together four or five solid seasons before you could even think about knocking heads with George Weiss, the Yankees' crusty general manager, and asking for top money—meaning $50,000 or so. I was fairly careful with what we had. We built a house in Commerce for $16,000 and I bought a new Lincoln. Merlyn's dad owned a lumberyard so we saved a bundle on the house.

If I had known that one day a collector would pay $55,000 for one of my jerseys at an auction, I would have hung on to more of the bats, home run balls, and World Series rings I gave away, some to family and friends, some to charity. What was a fellow to do with a dozen rings?

And I probably would have slept in that jersey.

It was like a reunion when the Yankees and the Dodgers returned for another Subway Series in '55. On paper, the odds favored us to keep it going. The Yankees had added some power in Moose Skowron, a first baseman, and Elston Howard, who could catch and play the outfield. With the arrival of Howard we had at last integrated the roster, eight years after the Dodgers brought up Robinson.

The pitching staff had undergone a remodeling. Whitey was now the main man, with Reynolds, Lopat, Sain, and Raschi all having moved on. Casey had traded for Bob Turley, Don Larsen, and Jim Konstanty, the ex-Phillies reliever, and brought back a veteran left-hander, Tommy Byrne, from the minors.

Turley and Larsen had been the key names in a huge, seventeen-player trade we made with the Orioles that was the talk of baseball in the spring. Gene Woodling was the only regular we gave up, but we sent seven players and two minor league prospects to Baltimore.

The Dodgers were nearly intact, with two crucial changes. After leading the club to two pennants and a tie in three years, Charlie Dressen demanded a long-term contract and his wife wrote Dodgers' owner Walter O'Malley a letter arguing his case. The Dodgers believed in one-year contracts and they didn't believe in wives writing letters. Dressen was replaced by Walter Alston, a successful manager in the Brooklyn farm system, and a career minor leaguer. He had one turn at bat in the majors and he struck out. He was unknown to the fans and the media, and when his hiring was announced one of the papers ran a headline that said: ALSTON (WHO HE?) TO MANAGE DODGERS. He would go on to sign twenty-three one-year contracts.

The other key change was the emergence of Don Newcombe as a twenty-game winner and the ace of their staff. He had pitched poorly in 1954 after two years in the army. The Dodgers had also added a hustling little Cuban outfielder named Sandy Amoros.

But there was a cloud over the Dodgers that October. This was their seventh trip to the World Series and they had lost them all, the last five to the Yankees. The fans in Brooklyn were always looking forward to next year. They were the most loyal, the most profane, and the most critical of any fans anywhere.

A best-selling book and movie had been written a few years earlier called *A Tree Grows in Brooklyn*. The last time we beat the Dodgers in the World Series, Dick Young, who covered them for the *Daily News*, wrote: "The tree that grows in Brooklyn is an apple tree. It grows apples in the throats of the Dodgers whenever the money is on the line."

Nothing the Dodgers did could undo this judgment, until they won the Series. They did everything else that season: got off to another blazing start with ten straight wins and twenty-two in their first twenty-four games. They led the National League in eleven hitting and pitching categories. Campanella was voted the league's Most Valuable Player for the third time in five years.

We had to scramble like mad to beat out the Indians and the White Sox in a three-way race. We might not have done it without the return of Billy Martin from the army for the final twenty games. He came in cold and hit .300

over that stretch. You could measure his value by the fact that we had finished second to Cleveland without him in 1954.

His return meant that the Three Musketeers had been reunited—Billy, Whitey, and me. Ford and Martin were friends when I joined the club. All we had in common was being young and wearing Yankee pinstripes, which meant we had everything in common.

Casey called Ford his "banty rooster," and the writers dubbed us "The Dead End Kids." Whitey was a joker in the clubhouse or in a bar, but on the field he was quiet and unsmiling. When Stengel was named the manager of the Yankees, he heard about this kid left-hander they had at Binghamton, Eddie Ford, and he asked one of their scouts about him. "It's funny you should ask," said the scout. "I was down there last week and he said to me, 'Doesn't that old bastard [meaning Stengel] know I could be up there right now, winning games for him?' "

The Yankees called him up from the minors in midseason of 1950, and early on he beat the Tigers, 8-1. The word was he had a wicked curve and he could throw it at three speeds. Yogi said he was curious to find out if the report was right, and for the first pitch of the game he gave the sign for a curve and held up his mitt. Whitey hit the pocket, and he continued to hit it for the next sixteen years.

I was having my best season when it happened to me again. I looked like a cinch to become the first Yankee to hit forty homers since DiMaggio in 1937. Then on September 16, while beating out a bunt, I suffered a severe muscle tear in the back of my right thigh. I made only two appearances the rest of the way, as a pinch hitter. Still, I led the American League in homers for the first time, with thirty-seven, eleven triples, and drove in ninety-nine runs. But, dammit, I was going into another World Series at less than full strength.

I missed the first two games and we won them both. In

the opener, Joe Collins homered twice in a 6-5 victory. The first one gave us a lead and the second made it safe. Joe was another guy who had been nicked up most of the season. I'm not making excuses. But I was probably more aware of injuries because they plagued my whole career.

Collins, a lean, supple guy from Scranton, Pennsylvania, wore a shin guard to protect a bruised leg and had been taped for a strained muscle in his groin. He also missed games with a virus and bad tonsils. He checked out of Lenox Hill Hospital one day in time to save a stranger's life with a home run in the tenth inning of a night game.

The stranger was watching the game on television in his home in Long Branch, New Jersey, when Joe broke it up. The man switched off the set and walked into the kitchen. Moments later, a runaway car came hurtling in from the street and shattered the television set. Some of us thought Joe should have got a Carnegie Medal, at least.

Ford was the winner in the opener, and we made it two in a row, 4-2, behind the pitching of Tommy Byrne. Neither of the Dodger starters, Don Newcombe and Billy Loes, was able to go six innings. The omens were looking good. Only four teams had ever won the World Series after trailing two games to none.

Byrne, pushing thirty-six, was topping off the best year of his career. Tommy was with the Yankees when Stengel took over in 1949, but he was traded to the Browns in 1951. He bounced around to Chicago and Washington and then went back to the minors before the Yankees decided they could use him again. He turned into the steadiest pitcher on the staff and had the best winning percentage in the American League, with sixteen victories and five losses. He stopped the Dodgers on five hits and drove in two runs with a bases-loaded single.

But we paid a price in Game 2. Hank Bauer joined me on the gimpy list, pulling a muscle. He would be available only for limited duty the next three games. We had two backups starting in the outfield, Bob Cerv and Elston Howard. Shortly before the third game at Ebbets Field I decided I could play.

It really hurt to lose Bauer, the toughest and strongest player I ever saw. He had muscles in his breath. He was an ex-marine, had fought the Japanese at Guadalcanal, and had a flat face with a nose spread wide. During batting practice the next day, a fan behind home plate called out to Whitey and demanded that he find Bauer, explaining they had served together in the marines. There was no reason to disbelieve him, since he had the same flat face as Hank.

Whitey watched the two of them talking and said, "Hot damn! What were those Japanese armed with? Shovels?"

With Bauer out, I went to Casey shortly before the third game at Ebbets Field and told him I thought I could play. I was all right until the game started. In the first inning, I chased down Carl Furillo's routine fly in right-center. I felt a burn in my thigh and I was really hobbling. I must have looked like Chester in the old *Gunsmoke* TV series by the time I reached the ball. The next inning Casey moved me to right field, Cerv from left to center, and Howard from right to left.

I stroked a homer off Johnny Podres my first time at bat in the Series, but that was about it. The Dodgers pounded Turley and all our pitchers and whipped us, 8-3. It was the twenty-third birthday for Podres, who was pitching with a sore arm and had not completed a game since mid-June. He had won only twice in his last thirteen starts.

I limped through Game 4 and that was about the end of my Series. Left-handers had won each of the first three games, but two right-handers, Don Larsen and Carl Erskine, started this one. In the fourth inning, home runs by Campanella and Hodges produced three runs and put the Dodgers ahead, 4-3. In the fifth, Duke Snider gave Brooklyn three more with a homer that dented an automobile in a parking lot across Bedford Avenue.

The Dodgers won, 8-5, and the Series was tied. The irony was that Casey would have walked Snider, if not for a mental lapse by our young relief pitcher, Johnny Kucks. He had relieved Larsen with a man on first and nobody out. The first man to face him, Pee Wee Reese, rapped a hard grounder that Collins fielded to his right. Kucks forgot to cover first base and by the time he broke for the bag Reese was safe. The next batter was Snider.

"If only Kucks had covered first and Reese was out," moaned Casey, "we'd have walked Snider and played for the double play. Instead, he gets his shot and hits the bejabbers out of it."

In Game 5 we made a hero out of a rookie pitcher named Roger Craig, who had been called up from St. Paul in July. A year earlier, he was pitching for Newport News in the Piedmont League. He held us to four hits and two runs, and Clem Labine came on to protect the win, 5-3. For the first time in their history, the Dodgers had taken three World Series games in a row. Our outfield had been stripped by injuries and our pitchers couldn't stop the Brooklyn bats. Sandy Amoros hit a homer and Snider knocked two more out of sight.

Years later, Craig would earn respect as a pitching coach and manager, and as the inventor of the split-finger fastball. But that day he was just a gawky rookie with wind flaps for ears, a kid from the red clay hills of North Carolina who humbled the New York Yankees.

When the teams moved back to the Bronx, Alston gambled on another rookie, Karl Spooner. Casey had to go with our money pitcher, Whitey Ford. Spooner faced six batters; five reached base and scored. The big blow was Moose Skowron's three-run homer and at the end of an inning the Yankees led, 5-0.

Whitey thrived on the pressure and the commotion of the World Series. He went the full nine, checked the Dodgers on four hits, struck out eight and set the stage for a seventh game with a 5-1 victory.

Ford was the best clutch pitcher I ever saw and one of the smartest. He was criticized for not finishing more games, but criticism didn't bother Whitey. He had a soreness in his shoulder for most of his career, and if he had a big lead he would come out of the game around the seventh inning. This way he could start again in four days instead of two weeks. If the score was close, he didn't come out. He just wouldn't.

He was the percentage pitcher. He won 69 percent of his games and Casey often passed up his turn against a weak team to save him for the tough ones. The tougher the opponent, the bigger the game, the better he was, in the regular season or in the World Series—especially the World Series. If he didn't beat you, he kept the Yankees close enough for somebody else to come in and beat you. Whitey's weakness was that he couldn't start every day.

The deciding game would be pitched by Johnny Podres and Tommy Byrne, the young and old southpaws, each with a win in his only start. The Yankee fans were still with us, but around the country the Dodgers were the sentimental favorites and nearly everybody seemed to be rooting for us to get beat. I don't mind telling you, that was a lousy feeling.

This was going to be a historic Series and it demanded a terrific pitcher's duel. That was what we got. Byrne started out with three hitless innings, but in the bottom of the third you got a sense that the breaks were not going to fall our way. With Rizzuto on second base and Martin on first with two out, Gil McDougald bounced a fair ball toward third so slowly he seemed sure to beat any play to first. But Rizzuto slid into the batted ball and was automatically out to end the inning.

In the previous three games at Yankee Stadium, Roy Campanella had not made a hit. His first was one of the biggest of his life, a double in the fourth inning that enabled him to score on Hodges's single, the only run Podres would need. Hodges drove in the other run with a sacrifice fly in the sixth to give the Dodgers their 2-0 lead.

In the bottom of the sixth, Alston made a defensive move, sending Sandy Amoros to left field in place of Junior Gilliam. Now we staged our most serious threat of the game. Martin walked and McDougald beat out a bunt to put runners at first and second with nobody out and Yogi Berra due up. There was no one I would rather see batting in that situation than Yogi, unless it was me.

He sliced a fly ball down the line in left field, far out of the reach of Amoros, who was playing Berra well over toward center, as he should have been. Except that the little Cuban kept coming and the ball wasn't out of his reach, after all. A little luck was involved. He made the catch because he threw left-handed. With the glove on his right hand, he stretched as far as he could and speared the ball near the stands. A right-handed outfielder would not have made that catch. He would have had to reach across his body and backhand the ball.

By the time McDougald realized Yogi's fly wasn't going to fall in for extra bases, Amoros had made the catch and was able to throw to Reese, who relayed it to Hodges at first for the double play. It was one of the more spectacular plays ever made in a World Series and it had to happen against us. That's how it went because that's how it was meant to go.

I popped up as a pinch hitter in the eighth. In the ninth, Skowron rapped one back to the mound. Cerv flied out to Amoros. Howard rolled out to short and the game was over. Podres had scattered eight hits to shut us out, 2-0. Was he sharp? He had two strikes on each of the last three batters, and all but one was called.

The crowd stayed on long after the players had left the park. The last I looked, little kids were running the bases, and measuring their shoes against the spike marks Podres had left in front of the mound. The Dodgers had done what had seemed for so long to be undoable and unthinkable. They had won their first World Championship.

It was fitting that Gil Hodges would drive in both runs,

repaying the fans for their support when he endured that awful 0 for 21 slump in 1953. It had to be a very emotional moment for their captain, Pee Wee Reese, who had been on the 1941 Dodger team that lost the Series when catcher Mickey Owen missed a third strike; and the '51 team that was shell-shocked by Bobby Thomson's home run.

Then there was Snider, who hit four homers and was all over the outfield picking off one howling line drive after another. That was when the debate began to really heat up, in the boroughs of New York, over which center fielder was the best: Mays, Mantle, or Snider, three future Hall of Famers. It was given a kind of permanence a couple decades later when Terry Cashman set it to music, with a song called, "Talkin' Baseball—Willie, Mickey, and the Duke."

That gave more meaning to the rivalry, and it gave the analysts a lot of ammunition. Measuring, weighing, comparing, baseball fans do it better than anybody. It probably boils down to a question of style. We each had our advantages. Willie stayed healthy and played in 749 more games than Duke, 591 more than I did. Snider played his first 10 years in Ebbets Field, a friendly park for home run hitters. For much of that time he was the only left-handed batter in the Dodger lineup, meaning that he had the left-right percentages in his favor much of the time. I had the benefit of switch-hitting and the speed to beat out bunts for base hits. Nor could teams pitch around any of us, given the power hitters up and down our batting orders.

I have been asked the question a thousand times at card shows—Which of us was the best? All you have to do is open the record book and the answer, over a full career, is Willie. He played twenty-two years to my eighteen. He finished with more of everything, including homers. In my prime years, head to head, I think I had the edge. I was faster and a better base stealer and we were about even defensively, although Mays, with his basket catches, had more of a flair. I'll give him that.

Of course, Dodger fans could always make a case for

Snider, who may have been the steadiest of the three. For five straight seasons in the 1950s, he averaged above .300 and he finished with 407 homers. When I saw Duke recently at a card show, he whispered in my ear, "Hey, Mantle, these golden years suck, don't they?"

"Actually, I've sort of enjoyed them," I said.

In a three-year period, you might get three different answers. *The Sporting News* did, picking Willie as the Major League Player of the Year in 1954, Snider in 1955, and me in 1956.

Over the years, people kept asking me another question: If the Yankees couldn't win the World Series, was I glad that the Dodgers finally did? The answer is, hell no. I'm a Yankee. I didn't want any other team to win the World Series.

But maybe in a tiny, hidden corner of my heart I was kind of happy for them, and especially for Sandy Amoros. That was his one shining moment in the big leagues.

There were two postscripts to the story of the 1955 fall classic, and the year the Dodgers finally won it all. Amoros played for them another season, then drifted out of the league and vanished. The next time I heard about him was in 1967. He had escaped from Cuba with his family. After several years of trying, Sandy, his wife, and their thirteen-year-old daughter had returned to the United States. They were hungry and penniless and free.

Buzzie Bavasi, the general manager of the Dodgers, read in the papers that he was back and he learned from John McHale, in the commissioner's office, that Sandy was seven days short of becoming a five-year man in the majors. The Dodgers had an open spot on their roster. So for one week in May of 1967, Sandy Amoros filled it.

He wouldn't go into the lineup as a late-inning defensive replacement because he was thirty-seven and hadn't played baseball in five years. But he wore a Dodger uniform and he would qualify for a pension that was worth $250 a month then, much more now. And to help him along, the

Dodgers paid him a full month's salary of $1,300. Castro's government had taken everything he had: a thirty-acre ranch, a few thousand dollars in the bank, and his car. He and his family lived on the pesos he had hidden in his home. Food had been hard to get. "Two pounds rice for month," he said. "One pound meat for two weeks. Beans? Two pounds a month." He moved to the village where he was born, and waited there, doing nothing, surviving, until the word came that he could take his wife and child to America. A friend in Miami had arranged a job for him through Catholic Charities in Brooklyn, which served as his sponsor.

For a week, at least, Amoros got to remember what it was like to be a big leaguer. And it happened because Bavasi remembered something more important than the running catch that saved the seventh game of the 1955 World Series. He remembered that Sandy Amoros was a human being and I admire the Dodgers for signing him to a contract and stirring up all the memories of what it was like when a ballclub grew in Brooklyn.

You know who else was almost a member of that team? Tommy Lasorda. In the spring he was a rookie left-hander fighting for his last chance to make the roster. In May, Walter Alston, the manager he would succeed twenty-two years later, gave him a start against the Cardinals. He walked two guys and he was working on the next hitter, whose name was Stan Musial. A pitch got away from Campanella. Another pitch got away and the runner on third came roaring home, a tough Texan named Wally Moon. Lasorda covered the plate and Moon hit him like a truck. The run scored.

Tommy went on to strike out Musial and Rip Repulski to get out of the inning. In the dugout they noticed his uniform was getting red around one knee. He was thinking that he had to make the club, he told me years later, and getting hurt was a mark against you. Back then, it was almost as bad as losing. They called the team doctor into the dugout and he looked at the knee. He told Tommy, "Son, if you try to pitch on that knee you may never pitch again." He had been spiked so badly that every tendon and ligament were exposed.

But Lasorda was thinking he had to pitch, he had to make the club. The next inning he started toward the mound, but two other players who heard the doctor grabbed him by the throat and held him back. "By the throat!" he said. "That's how I got taken out."

The date was May 5, 1955, and it was easy to remember because after the game the front office told him he was going back to the minors. Before he left, he went in to see Buzzie Bavasi and beg him for a chance to stay. Bavasi said, "Put yourself in my chair. Who would you send out?"

Tommy told him, "Hell, there's a kid left-hander on this club who can't even throw a goddamn strike." Bavasi said, maybe so, but the kid left-hander was paid a bonus to sign and the rule was that a bonus baby had to stick with the big club for two years or else you lost him.

The name of the bonus baby who couldn't throw a strike was Sandy Koufax. I remember hearing about him when we played the Dodgers in Vero Beach in the spring. He was so wild that they worked him out behind the minor league barracks, out of sight of the other players. He overcame his wildness, but by then the Dodgers were in Los Angeles and Lasorda was back in the minors.

"It hurt ten times worse than the spiking," he said, "being shipped out. But I always said, it took the greatest left-hander in history to get me off the Dodgers."

Tommy spent parts of two seasons in Brooklyn, appeared in eight games, and had no wins and no losses. I doubt that many fans know that Lasorda was picked up by the Kansas City A's in 1956, and had an 0 and 4 record before he was released. I remember it because he got into a nasty fight with Billy Martin.

I forget who was pitching for us, but he brushed back a couple of Kansas City players and their manager, Lou

Boudreau, was screaming so loud in the dugout we could hear him across the field. "That's what's wrong with this lousy club," he said. "Everyone is afraid of the Yankees."

Lasorda jumped up and said, "Put me in there!" He did and Tommy knocked down the first two hitters, then threw two pitches behind the head of Hank Bauer and two behind the head of Billy. Well, you can guess what happened next. Martin yelled something. Lasorda yelled back and—pow. The two of them went after each other like pit bulldogs.

In the middle of the action, Bauer tried to get at Lasorda, who shouted at him between punches: "Stay out of this, Bauer. This is an Italian fight." When the blood dried, Billy and Tommy shook hands and they became great pals.

Billy believed that a combative nature was part of the Yankee legacy and Casey loved him for it. Whenever the team was in a slump, or seemed to be getting lethargic or overconfident, the old man would walk over to Billy's locker and tell him to start a fight during the game that day.

The Yankees were involved in their share of brawls, but to be honest I never took part in them. I was a peacemaker, not a fighter. I tried to break them up. I'm not sure what held me back, but I know that DiMaggio never got into a fight in his career and neither did Lou Gehrig.

# THE PERFECT FINISH

## 1956—YANKEES 4, DODGERS 3

I had the year of my life in 1956, winning the Triple Crown and being voted Most Valuable Player in the American League. It was as if a three-hundred-pound gorilla had been removed from my back. Even Casey acted as though I had finally played up to my potential.

But there wasn't much danger that I would get a fat head because I had teammates like Yogi to keep me square. Before we met the Dodgers in the World Series that fall, for the fifth time in six years, Berra was interviewed for a radio show. The broadcaster said, "We're going to do free association. I'm going to throw out a few names and you just say the first thing that pops into your mind."

"Okay," said Yogi.

When they went on the air, the announcer said, "I'm here tonight with Yogi Berra and we're going to play free association. I'm going to mention a name and Yogi's just going to say the first thing that comes to mind. Okay, Yogi?"

"Okay."

"All right, here we go then. Mickey Mantle."

"What about him?" said Berra.

It wasn't an accident that the Yankees and the Dodgers kept meeting in the World Series. Each team had at least six regulars who had been together five years or more. We would add one or two rookies a season. How many teams do you think can say that of their lineups today, with guys jumping from club to club and grabbing those mega-million-dollar free agent contracts? Hey, I don't blame them. I'm just pointing out that you don't see teams sticking around long enough to develop that feeling of being a family.

We were going up against the Dodgers with the roles reversed. We were seeking revenge and trying to regain the World Championship. They were trying to defend it. And for the first time, I didn't care how I compared to Willie or Duke. I wasn't going to scuff my toe and say, aw shucks, it was nothin'.

I'm proud of what I accomplished in '56. I had a .353 batting average, 52 homers, and 130 runs batted in to lead the majors in all three categories. Only three men had done that before me: Rogers Hornsby, Lou Gehrig, and Ted Williams. I did it wearing a brace on my right knee. Almost as much as the MVP award, I appreciated what Cleveland's Early Wynn said to reporters about me after the All-Star Game: "I watched him dress. I watched him bandage that knee—that whole leg—and I saw what he had to go through every day to play. And now I'll never be able to praise him enough. Seeing those legs, his power becomes unbelievable."

It probably isn't good form to hide behind another player to pay yourself a compliment, but I think I'm entitled to that one. And I'll just leave it there.

With Berra, Bauer, and Skowron pounding the ball all summer, we hit 190 homers to break the single-season record set by the 1936 Yankees. But this is a game that never lets you get complacent, and that was demonstrated on the Yankees by the retirement of Phil (Scooter) Rizzuto and how it happened. He was the last link to the prime of Joe DiMaggio, but the Scooter had become a spare part with Gil McDougald switching to shortstop and a kid named Tony Kubek coming up behind him.

We were having a romp in the American League race, winning the pennant by nine games. The Dodgers had to go to the last day to finish ahead of Milwaukee, but Casey had the luxury of looking ahead and he figured we would be seeing the Brooklyn club again in October. He wanted another left-handed-hitting outfielder to send up against the Dodger pitching, and he had his eye on Enos Slaughter, the old Cardinal who had been with us for the final ten weeks of the 1954 season.

He was with Kansas City now and to make him eligible for the World Series roster the Yankees needed to acquire him before the first of September. A player had to be cut and this is how it was done.

Casey asked Rizzuto to drop by his office and when Phil got there George Weiss was also in the room. They explained that they had a chance to pick up Slaughter and made it appear they were asking Scooter for his opinion. Weiss showed him the roster and invited him to suggest a player who might be expendable. As he went down the list, he ruled out this name and that name. He pointed out an extra pitcher and catcher, but Casey explained why he needed them. Then it dawned on Rizzuto why he was really there. Before Weiss could inform him that the club intended to keep him on salary and restore him to the roster after the deadline, Scooter was gone. He went back to the clubhouse, took off his uniform, dressed, and left the stadium. His career as a Yankee, which included an MVP season in 1950, ended right there.

I felt badly for Rizzuto, but it was a classic Yankee move, signing the forty-year-old Slaughter. My boyhood idol was

Stan Musial, but Slaughter wasn't far behind. He got a kick of my telling him how I had rooted for him when I was in high school. Enos didn't start for us, but he hit .289 in twenty-four games and he could light a fire on the bench. There was a fight one day with the White Sox, and one of my all-time favorite photographs showed Slaughter walking off the field, his uniform shirt torn to shreds.

One reason the Yankees won so many pennants was their willingness to acquire a premium player for the stretch run. The likes of Mize, Slaughter, Sain, and Johnny Hopp all helped.

The Dodgers did some maneuvering of their own, adding thirty-nine-year-old Sal Maglie to a pitching staff that had lost Johnny Podres to military service. It was nearly winter for the boys of summer. Of the players who had been at the center of the team, only Snider was under thirty and he made it by one year. Robinson was thirty-seven and would retire after the Series. Campanella was turning thirty-five; Reese and Furillo were thirty-four. You might beat the Dodgers, but you didn't beat them because of their mistakes.

President Eisenhower and his secretary of state, John Foster Dulles, attended the opener at Ebbets Field, taking a break from the Suez Canal crisis, the Russian invasion of Hungary, and the 1956 election.

Maglie, who had won thirteen games for his new teammates, and Ford were the first-day starters. I tagged Sal for a two-run homer in the first inning over the screen in right field to quiet the crowd, but not for long. Robinson hit a bases-empty homer and Hodges connected with two on. Whitey lasted just three innings, Maglie went the distance and the Dodgers won, 6-3.

After a day of rain, the Yankees staked Don Larsen to a six-run lead, Berra's grand slam in the second inning chasing Don Newcombe from the mound. But in the bottom of the inning the Dodgers produced six runs to tie the game. Casey pulled Larsen, who had won eleven games for us with his unusual no-windup delivery, after he loaded the bases on a single and two walks. Kucks and Byrne came on before we could get off the field, and by then Snider's homer had accounted for half the runs.

In all, we used seven pitchers and they gave up twelve hits and eleven walks as the Dodgers dealt us more misery, 13-8. They got seven innings of steady relief from Don Bessent, whose nickname was The Weasel and whose big league career lasted less than four seasons. The game lasted three hours and twenty-eight minutes, and the second inning seemed to take up most of it.

We dragged our embarrassed selves back to Yankee Stadium, needing to regroup quickly. Casey turned once again to Ford, and Alston called on Roger Craig to keep the momentum going. The guy who picked us up and delivered us from evil was Enos Slaughter. The old warhorse whacked a three-run homer in the sixth inning, and along with a solo homer by Billy Martin, that was all the support Whitey needed. He went the full nine and put down the Dodgers, 5-3.

Slaughter's hot bat had been overlooked in our first two games, both losses. But not now. He was 7 for 12 for the Series, and the homer was his first in the World Series in ten years. The last time was against the Boston Red Sox on October 10, 1946, a baseball lifetime ago. That was the Series when Slaughter scored from first on a hit by Harry Walker to win the seventh game for the Cardinals. Enos said they had him running from first to home all winter on the banquet circuit. His last World Series homer in Yankee Stadium was in 1942, off Red Ruffing, a hero of another generation of Yankee fans.

And even more amazing, he was waiting for a phone call from his wife, Helen, who was expecting their baby any moment.

We were able to start breathing normally again after Game 4. Carl Erskine left the scene, trailing our young right-hander, Tom Sturdivant, after four. I led off the sixth with a homer to deep right-center off relief pitcher Ed Roebuck. Hank Bauer ripped one with a man on base off the big Dodger rookie, Don Drysdale, in the seventh. The final score was 6-2.

But the game belonged to Sturdivant, twenty-five, who was 1 and 3 as a rookie in 1955. In May they almost sent him back to the minors, but Casey gave him a couple starts and he went on to win sixteen games while losing eight.

Against the Dodgers, he let the leadoff batter reach base in each inning up to the seventh—on three walks, two hits, and an error. Twice Casey trudged crablike to the mound, and twice the crowd cheered his decision to let Sturdivant finish the job.

He proved again that there was no mess in baseball that couldn't be cured by neat pitching. After the first two games we looked like something that had been overlooked by the sanitation department. Now the Series was even and the best was yet to come. Everything that had happened up to then was just setting up a day of unbelievable perfection.

The edge for Game 5 seemed to rest with the Dodgers, who were coming back with Sal Maglie, who had gone the distance to beat us in the opener. Casey's choice was Larsen, who hadn't been able to hold a six-run lead in Game 2. His decision was quickly second-guessed.

Larsen was going to make Stengel look like a genius by pitching the first no-hit, no-run, no-man-reach-base game in the history of the World Series, the first perfect game in the major leagues in thirty-four years, twenty-seven up and twenty-seven down.

It kind of begs the obvious to say that Larsen was an odd candidate for immortality. He was one of the great night owls, a happy-go-lucky guy who drifted from team to team and would never win more than eleven games in a season. He had a record of 3 and 21 as recently as 1954 with the Baltimore Orioles. His manager in Baltimore, Jimmy

Dykes, said that Larsen "fears nothing in the world except a night's rest."

The biggest news he made in the spring was when he fell asleep at the wheel and wrapped his car around a tree. His wife had filed for divorce the morning of the game.

The Yankee Stadium crowd of nearly 65,000 was slow to sense what was happening. In the second inning, Jackie Robinson hit a sharp grounder to the left side that Andy Carey deflected to Gil McDougald, who threw from deep in the hole to nip Jackie by a step. The younger Jackie Robinson would have beat the throw with ease. That was the first of several close calls Larsen would have that day. In the fifth, Gil Hodges hit a drive to deep left-center, but I caught up with it at the last instant and made the grab over my shoulder—as good a catch as I ever made. The crowd let out a throaty roar.

That catch saved the perfect game and the next hitter, Sandy Amoros, hit a ball into the right-field seats—but just foul. So Brooklyn was robbed of two runs by the thinnest of margins.

For three innings neither team had a baserunner. Maglie retired the first eleven Yankees, but with two out in the fourth I fouled off several pitches on the outside corner, until he finally came inside. I hooked a line drive into the lower right-field stands for a home run for the first hit off Maglie.

Hank Bauer singled in a run in the sixth to give Larsen a 2-0 lead and now the whole show was his. When we came off the field after the top of the seventh, Billy Hunter politely asked me to move down the bench since Hunter had been sitting in that spot all afternoon. Larsen ducked into the runway for a smoke and when I walked by he asked, "Well, Mick, do you think I'll make it?"

I blinked but said nothing. This was contrary to the oldest superstition in baseball: you never refer to it if a pitcher is working on a no-hitter.

In the eighth, Larsen got Robinson, Hodges, and Amoros on easy outs. In the ninth, Carl Furillo fouled off four pitches then flied to right. Campanella hit a long foul, then rolled out to Martin at second. That brought up Dale Mitchell, a lifetime .314 hitter acquired from Cleveland, to bat for Maglie. He was the Dodgers' twenty-seventh and last chance.

By now I think everyone in the park was rooting for Larsen to get his perfect game—including the home plate umpire, Babe Pinelli. The count went to 2 and 2 and Larsen threw a fastball on the outside part of the plate. Pinelli seemed to take an extra split second, then raised his arm for strike three and the final out. I had a clear view from center field and, if I was under oath, I'd have to say the pitch looked like it was outside.

The moment produced another lasting image: Berra leaping into the arms of Larsen, who caught him at his waist. Our clubhouse was a zoo, except where Yogi sat. He bummed a cigarette from a writer, took a drag, looked up and said, "So. What's new?"

We still had one more game to win, but I'd have to say the celebration for Larsen rivaled any seventh-game victory party. This was a guy who hadn't done anything special until September, when he won four games and got rid of his windup. Don decided that, if all hitting was a matter of timing, why couldn't a pitcher unsettle the batter's rhythm by leaving out the big motion they were accustomed to seeing? Since then he just bent from the waist, straightened up, and threw. It certainly worked on this day.

Years later, a reporter asked him if he ever got tired of people asking him about the perfect game. "No," he replied. "Why should I?"

We now led three to two with the Series packing up and returning to Ebbets Field. The Dodgers figured to be shaken because you don't brush off a game that lands you on the dark side of the history books. But we were in for two surprises and both of them were bad.

Alston pulled Clem Labine out of the bull pen to start

the game, and he and Bob Turley traded goose eggs for nine innings. Labine went on to pitch a ten-inning shutout, and the last fellow to do that was Christy Mathewson.

The other surprise was more of an unwelcome reminder—that it's just a short hop from hero to bum. Slaughter had some fielding problems in left field, and one of them let in the only run of the game. With one out in the Dodger tenth, Junior Gilliam walked. Reese then sacrificed him to second, bringing up Duke Snider, who was given an intentional pass.

Now the hitter was Robinson, who had left five runners on base in his previous trips to the plate. He lined Turley's second pitch toward left and Slaughter, battling the sun and the shadows, started in. He realized his mistake, but he leaped too late. The ball was rising and it whistled over his glove and struck the wall. Gilliam raced home with the run that won it for Brooklyn, 1-0, and sent the World Series to a seventh game. The run was their first in nineteen innings.

Labine had started only three other games in 1956 and gone nine innings only once. Clem was not your typical jock. In his spare time he designed men's sports jackets. He had planned to teach history after he retired and he was a student of labor relations. He was also a hell of a competitor. He allowed seven hits and pitched out of trouble three or four times.

Turley deserved better. He pitched a four-hitter, struck out eleven, and allowed only two runners to reach base until Gilliam went all the way.

After the game, Billy Martin went up to Stengel on the team bus—I don't know anybody else who would have done this—and said, "If you're going to keep playing that National League bobo out there, we're going to blow the Series."

Casey, who had gotten used to Billy's brashness long ago, asked him calmly who Billy would play. "You better put Elston out there," he said, "and you better get Skowron's ass back on first base."

Stengel did just that for the seventh game. Elston hit a solo homer, Moose added a grand slam and Yogi rocked the Dodger starter, Don Newcombe, for a pair of two-run homers. Newcombe failed for the fifth time to win a World Series start, and the fans booed him out of the park. We won it, 9-0, and it isn't true that nobody noticed that Johnny Kucks pitched a three-hitter, but he didn't need to work nearly so hard.

If you have to get blown out, the seventh game of a World Series is probably the most embarrassing time you could pick. Some of the jokers in the press box pointed out that if the Dodgers hadn't actually shown up, the score would have been the same—officially, a team that forfeits loses by 9-0. The Yankees had recaptured the championship we had last held in 1953, and avenged the loss to the Dodgers a year ago.

You never have to wait long, or look far, to be reminded of how thin the line is between being a hero or a goat. Newcombe won twenty-seven games that year, but still hadn't won in the World Series. The fans and the writers had tagged him as a guy who couldn't win the big one. And yet, in 1951, he would have been the winning pitcher in baseball's most famous playoff game—if Bobby Thomson doesn't hit a homer off Ralph Branca.

The Yankees had made it all the way back and Casey was a genius again. I can still picture the clubhouse after the Dodgers won in 1955, with Billy Martin near tears, pointing at Stengel and telling the writers, "It's a shame for a great manager like that to have to lose."

As Casey put it himself, he managed good that year. But there was another factor in our comeback that needs to be mentioned. My injuries were less serious than they had been in other years and I had gotten smarter as a hitter. Luck accounted for the first and time—I was twenty-six—had taken care of the second. I was more aware of the strike zone. I laid off the bad pitches and struck out less often. I covered the plate better, adjusting to inside pitches and taking the outside ones the other way. I still turned my temper on myself, but I didn't blow up as much. I resorted less to punching walls and kicking water coolers.

There were times in my career when I was urged to bat entirely from the right side, but I always refused. My dad had worked too hard to make me a switch-hitter to change now. But I couldn't keep people from arguing about whether I would have been better off hitting just one way. When I first made the club, some of the Yankee brass felt I would do better in the long run as a left-handed batter, mainly because of the two steps you save running to first and my ability to drag bunt.

Later in my career, others, including Yogi, came to feel that I was more dangerous right-handed, partly because I didn't strike out as much. Also, I had more power to the opposite field. There was not much doubt that overall I was better batting right-handed. I had a lifetime average of nearly .350 from that side.

I flirted with Babe Ruth's home run pace that year, an experience that would come in handy in 1961, when I was able to give Roger Maris some support. I was eighteen homers ahead of the Babe at one point, but to make a real run at the record I needed a great start in September. Instead, I did the opposite. In the month's first ten days I failed to hit one out or even drive in a run, going five for thirty-three. Pressing too hard, I began to fall into old habits, tempted by pitches out of the strike zone.

I still had my sights on the Triple Crown and I was in a tight race with Ted Williams for the batting title. The Yankees and the Red Sox went head to head in a three-game series twice in the last ten days of the season. Yankee pitchers were tough on Ted, who went 3 for 23 in the combined games. I was 7 for 14 and finished at .353 to Ted's .345. My last hit was my fifty-second home run, off Bob Porterfield.

When it was over, Williams was quoted as saying: "If I

could run like that son of a bitch, I'd hit .400 every year."
He was one of my idols, and I admired him even more
because his hits were mostly line drives. He didn't get any
leg hits at all. But I'll tell you, with a bat in his hand Ted
Williams gave a concert.

I didn't exactly maintain my standards in the World
Series. I hit only .250, but four of my six hits went for extra
bases—three homers and a double. Slaughter batted .350
and kept us alive in Game 3; never mind that some blamed
his fielding for the loss in Game 6. I enjoyed being around
him, listening to his stories. I still do. Instead of playing in
the World Series every October, I hold a Fantasy Camp now
in Fort Lauderdale. Country Slaughter is one of the coaches.
He's eighty years old and he can still hit.

I was pleased for him when he was finally voted into
the Hall of Fame. He played twenty-one years and was the
only lifetime .300 hitter who had been excluded. Most people thought the voters kept Enos out because of a couple of
incidents that had been distorted involving him and Jackie
Robinson.

He was accused of deliberately spiking Robinson on a
play at first base. He also was supposedly involved in a
threatened St. Louis boycott the year Jackie broke in with
Brooklyn. Enos told me, told everyone who would listen,
that the threat not to play never happened. The talk started
when Dixie Walker told some of the Cardinals he had
asked the Dodgers to trade him. And they did. He admitted
spiking Robinson, but only because "he had his foot on my
base. That's the way I played."

When he made it to Cooperstown, it was interesting to
note that one of the players who lobbied for him was Larry
Doby, the first black to play in the American League.

It seems as if we hear this every time somebody retires or
a team changes its uniform, but an era really did end with
the '56 Series. We would not meet a team from Brooklyn
again in October. And I've never forgotten a headline that

ran in the old *Brooklyn Eagle*, when the Dodgers trailed three games to two in 1953: DO NOT FORSAKE US.

Of course, that was what happened. Robinson retired, Campanella's career ended when he skidded off an icy road in January of 1958, and so he wasn't with them that spring when the team belonged to the city of Los Angeles. When they pulled him out of the wreckage his neck was broken. There was not much reason to believe he would live.

It was Campanella who said, "Baseball is a man's game, but you have to have a lot of little boy in you to play it." I never saw him when he wasn't upbeat, but Campy wasn't the type to complain or to reveal his private side. A friend said he was thinking about one of his sons, who had gotten into trouble, the night he lost control of his car. The years to follow were hard and painful. His first wife couldn't handle the stress of caring for a quadriplegic, and they were divorced.

He had to fight off the early depression. I heard about how he visited a hospital and apologized to a small boy for not being able to sign an autograph. "I'm paralyzed," said Campy. "That's all right," said the boy. "I'm blind." The ex-catcher learned, he coped, and he shared the lessons of a brave life up until his death in 1993, at the age of seventy-one.

The changes in the Yankees were less dramatic. In three of our four wins, the pitchers had been unfamiliar names: Sturdivant, Larsen, and Kucks. Yogi was in his prime, I was just coming into my own, Martin was born to lead, and Skowron, McDougald, and Howard were proving what they could do. We weren't "Murderer's Row" anymore, but the Yankees would still live and die with the long ball.

# A BRAVE NEW WORLD

## 1957—BRAVES 4, YANKEES 3

The fans who kept hoping for new faces in the World Series got half their wish in 1957. The Yankees would meet the Braves, who had won their first National League pennant for Milwaukee, all but sending the city into orbit.

The sad part for me was not having Billy Martin with us. He had been traded in June to the Kansas City A's after the so-called brawl at the Copacabana that became a part of the history of those Yankee years. The move hastened the makeover of the team, changed how I felt about the game, and cut way down on how much I partied during the season.

What didn't change was the regularity with which the Yankees still went to the World Series.

The punch line to the whole story was that Billy had little or nothing to do with the incident itself. Whitey Ford and I came up with the idea of inviting a few of the fellows, Yogi, Hank Bauer, Gil McDougald, Johnny Kucks, and their wives, to celebrate Billy's twenty-ninth birthday on the night of May 15 (a day early). We had dinner at Danny's Hideaway and then someone said we had time to catch Sammy Davis, Jr., at the Copa. We hailed some cabs and hustled over.

I can swear on a bible that whatever happened that night, it didn't compare to some of the scrapes Billy got into later as a manager with the Yankees and the Oakland A's. The Copa arranged a special table for us and sitting at a table near us was another party, members of a bowling team from the Bronx. We ordered a round of drinks and sat back to watch the show.

Davis was great, as he always was. But the bowlers were heckling him, and the language started getting loud and rough. Among the less vulgar references we heard was the phrase, "Little Black Sambo." Bauer, the ex-Marine, tried to quiet them down and they recognized us and now they started giving our table a hard time. Billy said why didn't they just give the whole audience a break and settle down and that started it. A bowler, who turned out to own a deli, staggered to his feet and invited Billy to step outside.

When Billy got up, Hank asked him where he was going and Billy said, "I'm just going to talk to him." The two of them followed the bowler toward the door, and the rest of us were right behind them. I tossed my napkin on the table and told Merlyn, "I better see that Billy doesn't get into trouble."

The next thing I heard was a loud crash, and one of the bowlers was sprawled on the floor by the cloakroom, out cold. I didn't see who hit him, but Whitey and I never lost sight of Hank and Billy and it wasn't either one of them. They were still in front of us. We figured that a couple of the Copa bouncers had grabbed the first guy and worked him over with a sap. By the time we got near him it looked like he had been hit ten or fifteen times.

We were hustled through the kitchen and out a side

exit that led into the lobby of the Hotel Fourteen. We led our bewildered wives into the street and piled into some cabs and got out of there. But the next day the story was headline news in the New York papers. Six of us—Ford, Martin, Berra, Bauer, McDougald, and myself—were fined $1,000 each by George Weiss. He let off Kucks for $500 because he was a rookie. What was worse, we all had to testify before a grand jury, which dropped the charges, and the deli owner filed a civil suit claiming that Hank had assaulted him, which was untrue. Yogi put it best in his testimony: "Nobody did nothin' to nobody." Except maybe the bouncers.

Casey disciplined us in his own way. Ford had been scheduled to pitch the next night against the A's, but he wound up pitching batting practice, with Bob Turley starting in his place. Billy was on the bench, but he had been banged up some to open the season and the rookie, Bobby Richardson, was already filling in at second base. Bauer played but was dropped to the eighth spot in the batting order. I played and hit third.

"I'm mad at him, too, for being out late," Casey said, referring to me, "but I'm not mad enough to lose the pennant over it."

I hit a homer into the left-field seats for the first run—I had reached base eleven times in my last twelve at bats. We went on to win the game behind Turley, who pitched a four-hit shutout and started a triple play. But the incident gave Weiss, who was never a fan of Billy Martin, an excuse to trade him to Kansas City.

Stengel broke the news to him. He called Billy into his office and told him, his voice low and raspy, "Well, you're gone. You're the best little player I ever had. You did everything I ever asked."

Billy couldn't forgive Casey for not somehow stopping the trade. He saw it as a question of loyalty, of sticking up for him. He went to the Athletics with Ralph Terry for Harry "Suitcase" Simpson and Ryne Duren. It was the second major trade we made that year with the A's. In the off-season, we made another of those jumbo swaps, giving up six players, including Irv Noren, Billy Hunter, and Tom Morgan, for pitchers Art Ditmar and Bobby Shantz, and Clete Boyer, who was then a minor league prospect at third base.

I honestly don't think Casey knew the deal had been made until Weiss told him. Anyway, they didn't speak for most of the next three years. Billy was passed on to Detroit and Cleveland, and when the Indians were at Yankee Stadium one day I grabbed him before a game and led him over to our dugout. I said, "Look, you're a lot younger than he is and one of these days he'll be gone and you'll regret it."

Billy had tears in his eyes and he was crying, and the old man had tears in his eyes and he was starting to cry. I even had tears in my eyes, too, and I was crying.

Casey and his wife, Edna, were childless, and while it's easy to overanalyze these things I know that on some level they looked on Billy, Whitey, Yogi, and me as their sons. I know he was a father figure for me a lot of years after my dad died. He had managed Billy in the minors, turned him into a more than respectable infielder, and truly loved him; Billy, who was so direct and sassy and just had no bullshit in him. I named my third son after him.

And Stengel was wise and shrewd enough to see in Yogi what others missed, a sensitive fellow who was often hurt by the jokes made about him, but smiled his way through them. I don't think he ever gave Berra anything but praise and encouragement. It took a while, but in time others in the organization came to understand what Yogi meant to the Yankees.

Whitey endeared himself with his cockiness and his consistency. I guess I filled the role of the son who was never quite going to live up to all the expectations. I don't remember this, but Billy said he once saw Casey grab me by the back of the neck and shake me after I had done something he didn't like, and he said, "Don't let me see you do that again, you little bastard!"

If it happened, that was okay, because Casey called all of us little bastards. He was referring more to our ages than our sizes. You didn't think of the old man as being big or small, but he was always vain about his body. Time and baseball had shrunk him some over the years, and his legs were curved and he walked with a stoop. But he was a thing of beauty to the photographers, and I wish I had a dollar for every time Casey mugged it up for the camera.

Trading Billy handed the job at second base to Richardson, and put a little more attention on the fact that the Yankees were bringing along their largest class of rookies in years. The group included Tony Kubek, Norm Siebern, Jerry Lumpe, Marv Throneberry, and Ralph Terry.

Still, I was blue sick about the deal because it was clear that the front office got rid of Martin partly because they thought he was a bad influence on me. I didn't subscribe to that theory because I had my best year rooming with Billy in 1956, at the Hotel St. Moritz, across from Central Park. We would wait on the corner at Fifty-ninth Street and Sixth Avenue for the team bus to pick us up for the trip to Brooklyn, during the World Series.

By then a lot of people knew my face, and Billy's. But we just stood there and waited and people walked around us, maybe with a glance here and there. I think back to that image of Billy and me standing on the corner of Sixth Avenue, talking, swinging aboard the bus, and nobody troubling us. You couldn't do that today, not in New York, not anywhere.

I never thought hanging out with Billy hurt me, but I was always more of a follower than a leader. I was drawn to his street smarts and his raw honesty. We were so close that Billy lived with Merlyn and me in Oklahoma the winter he went through his divorce. I missed Billy in 1957 and I miss him today.

The Yankees missed him, too. They had the most abundant farm system in baseball, although the Dodgers would overtake them after their move to Los Angeles. So they rarely hesitated to give up several for the few who might fill a special need.

They let one guy get away who had been in camp my rookie year, and we would meet up with him again in that fall of '57. He was Lew Burdette, and the Yankees tossed him into the deal when Casey decided that he had to have Johnny Sain for the pennant drive in 1952.

There was no way we would take the Braves lightly. They had a great ballclub: Hank Aaron, Eddie Mathews, Red Schoendienst, Warren Spahn, Burdette. The city of Milwaukee had gone wild over them. The players couldn't pick up a check anywhere—free groceries, free laundry, free beer.

I was especially eager to watch Aaron swing the bat. He was easily the most underrated player of my time, which may sound like a strange thing to say about a guy who would break Babe Ruth's career home run record and become the new King of Swat.

But until then you really didn't read or hear much about him. Not until he collected his six hundredth homer in 1972, at the age of thirty-seven, did the press and fans catch on to what his opponents had always known: that Henry was one of a kind. He had three things going against him: (1) He didn't play in New York or Los Angeles; (2) he was too predictable, meaning that he would get his thirty or forty homers a year, hit .320 or so, and drive in over a hundred runs; and (3) he lacked showmanship. His cap didn't fly off when he caught a fly ball and after a game you never saw him eat twenty hot dogs and wash them down with two six-packs of beer.

He had the quickest wrists I ever saw. Baseball scouts talked about Aaron's wrists the way male moviegoers of another time talked about Betty Grable's legs. But what impressed me most about him was how stable he was. With the possible exception of Stan Musial, nobody played twenty years in the majors and changed less than Aaron.

One story came out of that World Series that revealed something about his nature. Yogi noticed that Aaron held the bat in a way that violated a long-held baseball position. "Hey," said Berra, from his squat, always willing to engage opposing hitters in friendly talk, "you got the bat facing the wrong way. Turn it around so you can see the trademark."

The standard belief was that if you hit the ball on the trademark you were more likely to crack your bat. I never questioned that theory and don't know of any hitters who did.

But Henry continued to stare at the mound. Out of the side of his mouth, he said, "Didn't come up here to read. Came up here to hit."

Other players would marvel when they heard that Aaron actually hit cross-handed when he signed as a teenager with the Indianapolis Clowns in the Negro Leagues. That is like playing a piano in handcuffs. His first day in spring training, he began ripping hits all over the field and the manager asked him why he gripped the bat the way he did. Henry said it was the only way he knew. They changed his grip to the conventional way and he went right on hitting line drives. The adjustment took maybe five minutes.

I admired everything I knew about him. His natural caution was sometimes taken for distrust. But Aaron was just a private person and he never confused chatter with conversation.

The Yankees were odds-on favorites to win the Series. As much as I missed Billy after hours, the team didn't miss a beat, socking away another pennant by eight games. I won my second straight MVP award, went for the fences a little less (34 homers) and hit for my highest average ever, .365. But Ted Williams turned the tables to win the batting title with .388. He fell just twelve hits short of .400.

A crowd of around 69,000 turned out to watch two

great left-handers face off in the first game, Whitey Ford and Warren Spahn. Our ex-marines, Bauer and Jerry Coleman, drove in two of the runs that made Ford a 3-1 winner. Bauer doubled home Coleman to break a scoreless tie in the fifth. An inning later, Andy Carey singled to bring in Elston Howard and send Spahn to an early shower. The Braves trailed, 2-0, but their manager, Fred Haney, knew that runs would be scarce.

Coleman greeted the new pitcher, Ernie Johnson, with a squeeze bunt that sent Berra sliding home in a cloud of dust from third. With his thick body, Yogi's quickness was always a surprise, and he had scored before Johnson could even field the ball.

Whitey was his usual efficient self the rest of the way, holding the Braves to five hits. He walked the first two batters in the top of the sixth, then struck out Aaron, got Joe Adcock on a dribbler to Howard at first, and struck out Andy Pafko. The last time the Chicago Cubs had appeared in a World Series, against the Tigers in 1945, Pafko was in their outfield.

I beat out two infield singles, proving that my legs were still functioning.

Coleman, a veteran of two wars and six pennant races, was playing his last season. He didn't know he was starting at second base until he saw his name in the lineup in the morning papers. In Stengel's platoon system, all of our infielders could fill in at second, short, or third. The way Casey moved people around, it was like being three deep at each position.

We lost Skowron for the Series when he reinjured his back, but Howard, Collins, and Suitcase Simpson were all licensed to play first base.

Game 2 was going to be especially interesting because we were going to see Burdette, the one-time Yankee farmhand who had won seventeen games for the Braves. All through his career, Lew was accused of throwing a spitter and everyone joked about it. He even threw them in practice games in spring training. He was the only pitcher I couldn't hit in 1951 when we trained in Arizona, and I knew what he was doing.

I also couldn't believe the Yankees let him get away. That spring he pitched nineteen innings and gave up only one run. No team could touch him.

We didn't do much better as the Braves tied the Series at a game apiece, getting all of their runs off Bobby Shantz in a 4-2 victory. When Bobby won twenty-four games for the pitiful Philadelphia A's in 1952, before he broke his left arm, he was their best pitcher, hitter, and fielder. The little left-hander looked like a half-grown boy, but he always gave you everything he had and he did this day. It just wasn't enough.

Hank Bauer's homer had matched one by Johnny Logan and tied the score at 2-2, but in the fourth the Braves chased Shantz. They scored twice on three straight hits and an error by Kubek before anyone was retired. We didn't give Bobby much help. I misplayed a triple by Aaron and he scored their first run on a single by Adcock, which I bobbled for an error, letting him take an extra base.

Except for Bauer's homer and a run-scoring scratch single by Coleman, we could do little against Burdette. The last six innings only one Yankee reached third base. He threw some nasty pitches. I can't say for certain that any of them were spitters, but as Red Smith wrote, Lew was the only player in the big leagues whose pitching record included three columns—"won, lost, and relative humidity."

The fans were going wild in Milwaukee as the teams took an off day to move to the Wisconsin cheeselands. The town was all dressed up with flags, buntings, and parades. A headline in the morning paper said: TODAY WE MAKE HISTORY. Hotels were jammed. Many of the fans had traveled for days to see the home team play in its first World Series, and many of them spent the night outdoors in sleeping bags. Even in the 1950s, that would not have been a good idea in New York.

When we got to County Stadium you could feel the sharp teeth of autumn and great, puffy white clouds were riding across a blue and sunny sky. There were reports of a bitter cold wave moving east from the Great Plains. On the steps of the dugout before the game, Casey turned to me and said, "Lookit them flags blowing straight up. There will be fly balls today that won't ever come down."

His prediction was on target and we were the ones hitting most of those flies. Both starters, Bob Buhl and Bob Turley, were gone after an inning and a half. The deeper you get into the Series, and on a day when the wind is blowing a gale, managers are not real patient with their pitchers.

The Braves used six and we stomped on them by a score of 12-3, the win going to Don Larsen with seven-plus innings of good relief work. Tony Kubek, the hometown boy, had three of our hits and two homers, driving in four runs. Tony was all the Milwaukee fans had to cheer about and he was on the wrong team.

I had two hits, including a two-run homer that landed in the bull pen in right-center in the fourth. By then, I was a medical case again. I get tired of bringing up injuries because so often they sound like excuses. But this is what happened: In the first inning, Bauer bounced out, Kubek hit his first homer over the right-field wall, I walked, and Berra walked. Taking a lead off second base, I stumbled and fell to my knees, then scrambled back to the bag as Buhl spun around and tried to pick me off. His throw sailed into center field and when Red Schoendienst leaped for the ball, his full weight fell on my right shoulder like a sack of cement. I got through the game okay and played in the next two, but I couldn't swing the bat freely and the shoulder nagged at me for years. I hit my homer batting left-handed against Gene Conley, but I would never again hit with the same power from that side.

I dug myself out from under Red and ran to third, with Berra beating the throw to second. I scored on McDougald's fly to Aaron and Yogi came across on Simpson's single. Milwaukee was down by three runs before a Brave had picked up a bat.

The Braves were blessed in Game 4, which was the famous "shoe shine" game. They took a 4-1 lead behind Spahn on homers by Aaron and Frank Torre in the fourth inning off Tom Sturdivant. Spahn was one pitch away from victory in the ninth, when Elston Howard, with two out and the count full, hit a three-run homer to send the game into extra innings.

In the tenth, Kubek beat out an infield single and Bauer scored him with a triple off the left-field fence. The Yankees led, 5-4. The game wasn't over, much less the World Series, but at that moment a lot of the fun had gone out of it for the Milwaukee fans.

Then they got a life when Tommy Byrne threw a low pitch to Vernal "Nippy" Jones, pinch-hitting for Spahn to lead off the bottom of the tenth. Jones claimed that the ball hit his right foot, but the umpire, Augie Donatelli, ignored him.

This was one of those moments where you think about the way fate works. Some athletes play an entire career without ever enjoying a taste of glory. Jones was one of those, a journeyman who had been brought up from Sacramento during the season because Joe Adcock broke his leg. He had pinch-hit for the Cardinals in the 1946 World Series and had been their regular first baseman for a brief time.

While Jones argued with Donatelli, the ball, which had struck the wall behind home plate and rebounded, rolled slowly between the two of them. Jones looked down, saw a black spot on the ball, picked it up and pointing, shouted in triumph to Donatelli: "It's the polish off my shoe!"

Donatelli gave in, Jones was waved to first and replaced by a pinch runner, Felix Mantilla. It happened so fast that Casey didn't have time to complain, and he still didn't after we lost, in a finish so dramatic that I bet most of Old Milwaukee woke up with a big hangover the next day.

Bob Grim came in to relieve Tommy Byrne, and Schoendienst bunted Mantilla to second. He scored from there on Logan's double to tie the game at 5-5. Then Eddie Mathews hit a tall home run into the gap between the fence and the bleacher seats in right field to end it, 7-5.

Mathews was the hero, but Jones had his instant of glory, even though being a hit batsman is a kind of drab, negative fact. I guess we were the first team in the history of the World Series, maybe in all of baseball, to get beat by a can of Shinola. If there is a moral here, it must be that it pays to be well-groomed. If you don't play much you have lots of time to shine your shoes.

The Series was square again at two apiece. I had gone 0 for 5 and the next day my bum shoulder put me on the bench. The Braves came back with Burdette and he shut us out, 1-0, Joe Adcock's single in the sixth driving in the only run off Ford.

It seemed to us that the Braves were winning with spit and polish. The Series went back to Yankee Stadium with Milwaukee needing just one more win to close us out.

Bob Turley kept us in the hunt by picking up his first World Series victory, 3-2, with home runs accounting for all the scores. Aaron and Frank Torre hit theirs with the bases empty. The Yankees won because Yogi smacked one in the third inning off Bob Buhl, with Enos Slaughter on base. But it was Bauer's solo homer off Ernie Johnson that broke a 2-all tie in the seventh.

Turley pitched his specialty, a four-hitter. He had lost one in ten innings to the Dodgers in 1956. Like Larsen, Turley worked without a windup. Instead, he took a deep breath before each pitch, and turned back the Braves with a mixture of high, hard stuff and curves.

Now everything came down to Game 7, with Larsen starting for us and Burdette, having gone eighteen innings in four days, trying again on two days of rest. I was back in the lineup for this one, and Skowron came off the bench to pinch-hit and stay in the game, but none of it mattered.

Lew did it to us again, spacing seven hits to get his second shutout and third win in six days, 5-0, as the Braves ended the eastern monopoly on the World Series. He really stuck it to us, finishing with twenty-four scoreless innings going back to Game 2. To find a better display of pitching under pressure, you had to go back to 1905, when Christy Mathewson had three shutouts and twenty-seven runless innings.

A wild throw by Kubek, on a double-play ball, left the stockyard gate unlocked, and the Braves scored four times on five hits in the third inning. But no one blamed the loss on Tony, the brightest rookie on the Yankee team. The Braves needed only one honest run and they got it on a homer by Del Crandall, the catcher, in the eighth inning off Byrne, the last of five Yankee pitchers.

We loaded the bases in the bottom of the ninth with two out on singles by McDougald, Coleman, and Byrne, a good hitting pitcher. But Mathews made a terrific play on Skowron's smash down the line and stepped on third for the force-out to end the game. It didn't matter that the Braves went into this one with a team batting average of .199. They had Burdette, and he found a real convincing way to remind the Yankees that they had let him get away. His control was what really surprised us. We didn't believe anyone could be so consistent at catching strikes on low pitches. We thought we could wait him out on his low stuff, and make him come up when he got behind on the count. We were wrong.

The way he dominated us proved two points that I believed in. One is that, unlike the regular season, pitching isn't 75 percent of the World Series but 90 percent. The other is that the so-called book on hitters means very little in such a short competition. Yogi told our pitchers, "Don't fool around, give me your best pitch." Every pitcher has to rely on what has been most effective in a jam, and the hitter knows what that pitch is. So it boils down to that very basic duel. And this time the Braves' pitching was best.

As a franchise, the Braves had last won a World Series in Boston in 1914, so they were sort of overdue. For the fans in New York, the significance went even deeper. The city was losing more than a championship. The Dodgers and the Giants were heading west, to Los Angeles and San Francisco, for the 1958 season. It was strange that spring to go into Vero Beach, where the Dodgers trained, and see the writers from Los Angeles, carrying their new typewriter cases, and the old beat reporters from New York and Brooklyn, on their last stories, arguing and resentful and getting in each other's way.

And the truth is, it started with Lou Perini, who owned the Braves and moved them from Boston to Milwaukee, although I doubt he realized what his move would do to the sports geography of the country.

Perini wasn't trying to be important. He just wanted to see his ballclub survive, and it couldn't do that in Boston, where he and his brothers were losing their shirts. They were in the construction business, and the papers referred to them as "The Three Steam Shovels."

So Perini decided to make the switch in 1953, hoping that the move into a new market would provide the profits that they could no longer earn competing against the Red Sox. The fans of Wisconsin went daffy over the Braves, and soon they were breaking the attendance records in the National League by selling two million tickets in a season.

The world's most interested observer of this development was Walter O'Malley, sitting in Brooklyn, where his team went to the World Series year after year and drew a million to a small and elderly ballpark. He figured, if the Dodgers draw a million and Perini continues to draw two, Milwaukee will soon have the best farm system, all the players, and all the pennants.

This was before the draft and before free agency and the only thing in baseball that did more talking than Casey Stengel was money. So that's why O'Malley made his deal in Los Angeles, in order to keep pace with the Braves in Milwaukee.

The Giants joined the Dodgers in California and that led to expansion in both leagues, and the birth of a team in New York called the Mets. Change happens, sometimes by accident and sometimes by plan. But it was an inadvertent move by Perini and the sunburst of support from the fans in Milwaukee that triggered the boom in sports.

But on the day the Braves took the title back to Wisconsin, no one was spending much time looking into crystal balls. They were too busy celebrating their victory and the performance of Lew Burdette. I knew from our spring camp as rookies in Arizona, when he wouldn't throw me anything good to hit even in practice games, that this was a tough customer who was always in command.

And years later, Bob Uecker, who was then the backup catcher to Crandall, told a story that gave another insight into Lew. A couple of hitters had reached base with none out, and Uecker went to the mound to check in with him.

When he got there, Burdette barked at him, "What the hell do you want?"

Uecker said, "Nothing. I just came out to give you a break."

Lew gave him a cold stare and said, "Don't be coming out here. They"—and he waved his gloved hand at the crowd—"think you're giving me advice. And the only thing you know about pitching is that you can't hit it."

I can assure you, Lew put some doubt in the minds of the Yankees, too, in 1957.

# COMING FROM BEHIND

## 1958—YANKEES 4, BRAVES 3

This may not have been the winter of my discontent, but it wasn't one of my best, either. I had surgery on my right shoulder to have whatever was torn in there repaired. George Weiss tried to cut my salary by $5,000 because he said my 1957 season wasn't as good as '56, when all I did was win the Triple Crown. The shoulder still was weak when I reported to spring training in 1958, the ache in my right knee would never go away and I developed shin splints.

But I had to play in all of the games because the team considered me a drawing card, and the clubs didn't like to lose money even in the spring. I understood that, and I felt an obligation to the fans who had taken time off from their jobs to travel to Florida and see the big leaguers in action. They were disappointed if their favorite players weren't in the lineup, and if that included me then I wanted to play.

None of this was what really made my winter a bummer. It was losing to the Braves. When I talked with Yogi or Hank or Moose or Whitey, we always got around to it. This shouldn't surprise anybody. No matter how much money you make, or how much fame you fall into, if you consider yourself a competitor you don't like to lose. You don't like to be embarrassed.

That part of the game hasn't changed. In 1993 there were forty players making over $4 million a year, and on opening day every one of them was thinking about the World Series, not their paychecks. Okay, it is easier not to think about it when you make $4 million a year, instead of $75,000, which was close to the ceiling in 1958. But I try to avoid that trap. Someone once told me that anytime you see a sentence that starts out, "In my day," or "way back then," ignore it. The golden age of anybody is when you were a kid and had all the answers, never mind the questions.

So the Yankees wanted another crack at the Braves and we got our wish in October. The Braves repeated in the National League, finishing eight games ahead of the surprising Pirates. There was no slippage in their pitching. Spahn won twenty-two games and Burdette won twenty.

Both Yogi and I got off to slow starts; by the end of May I had only four homers. But the club raced off to a 25 and 6 record so I can't claim that either one of us was indispensable. At one point, we led the field by seventeen games and wound up clinching the pennant on September 14 in Kansas City. The White Sox came in second, ten games back.

I led the league in homers again, with 42, 127 runs scored, 129 walks, and strikeouts, breaking the club record with 120. The bad right shoulder kept me from getting around on the fastball up and inside. When it comes to spotting a weakness and taking advantage of it, pitchers are like vultures, all of them.

I hit .304, and in a year when batting averages were down around the league, mine was respectable.

Although the Yankees had this image of being like a machine, or even General Motors, it didn't look that way from the inside. The '58 season was a winding road, kind of offbeat, as many of our seasons were.

In late summer, the front office hired a couple of Keystone Kops to follow the players on the road, which really pissed me off. Not that we didn't deserve to be followed. But they had gotten rid of Billy Martin because they thought he was leading us astray. So Billy was gone and how did it look now, with the club hiring two private detectives to tail us?

It was funny and stupid and a waste of money. If Casey wanted to know if the players were hitting the night spots and breaking curfew, all he did was tip the elevator operator, give him a new baseball, and tell him to ask for the autographs of each player who came in after midnight. The next morning he checked the ball and he had all the evidence he needed.

One night in 1958, I was going to dinner with Whitey and Darrell Johnson, our third-string catcher, and we saw the sleuths watching us in the lobby, peeking over their newspapers, just like in the movies. We decided to give them the slip and they wound up following Tony Kubek, Bobby Shantz, and Bobby Richardson—probably the three cleanest-living guys on the team—to the YMCA.

When we grumbled and joked about it in the clubhouse, Casey consoled us with a story about his own antics as a night owl, when he was an outfielder with the Giants under John McGraw. The Giants hired a private eye to snoop after Casey and Bob "Irish" Meusel. Casey went to McGraw and said, "I don't deserve this kind of treatment."

"Exactly what kind of treatment do you think you deserve?" McGraw snapped at him.

"It's the principle of the thing," Casey told him. "I got a right to have a whole detective to myself."

I broke out of my slump in June and in a period of less

than a month had three inside-the-park homers. Those are rare. I mean, whole teams go through a season without one. But I was puzzled myself because I knew how bad my knees were. If we rode in a cab for more than eight minutes, the other guys had to help me get out. And, yet, it didn't appear that I had lost any speed getting to first or running the bases. Then I figured it out. I had no problem running at full throttle, it was trying to stop or cut that gave me a fit.

I hit my twentieth homer on July 5 off Dave Sisler of Boston—the son of Hall of Famer George Sisler—in Yankee Stadium, and I remember because neither team won the game. My homer tied the game at 3-3 in the bottom of the ninth, and the Red Sox loaded the bases in the eleventh inning. At that point, over the public address system, it was announced that "this game must stop at 11:59," as no game starting on a Saturday night could go into Sunday morning.

This was one of those rules that baseball adopted a hundred years ago to satisfy the Pilgrims or somebody, and it probably came up twice in a decade.

But the Red Sox scored twice that inning and we began stalling. We argued calls, changed pitchers, switched infielders, called time to tie our shoelaces. Geez, everything just suddenly slipped into slow motion. And, sure enough, the game had to be called at 11:59 with the Red Sox still batting. Since the home team had not gotten its turn, the score reverted to a 3-3 tie and the game had to be replayed. However, all the individual records counted, including my game-saving home run.

There was some justice to that because they owed me one. After the game, Sisler recalled getting his first big league win after a homer had been taken away from me. "It looked to me like a home run," Sisler said. "The umpire at second base ruled that it made almost a straight, vertical drop and landed on top of the wall and came back in the park. The Yankees were furious." Now we were even.

In the All-Star Game in Baltimore, I started in center, flanked by Bob Cerv of the A's and Jackie Jensen of the Red Sox. I'm not sure if anyone else was aware of it, but that was a really interesting reunion. We had been the three young candidates to succeed Joe DiMaggio in 1952 as the Yankee center fielder.

The day after the All-Star Game, a number of baseball people appeared at a hearing before the Senate Subcommitee on Antitrust and Monopoly. Baseball was seeking an exemption from the antitrust laws, and though neither one of us had a clue what it was about Casey and I were among those called to testify. This is an excerpt of what Stengel told the senators.

SENATOR ESTES KEFAUVER: Mr. Stengel, you are the manager of the New York Yankees. Will you give us very briefly your background and your views about this legislation?

STENGEL: Well, I started in professional ball in 1910. I have been in professional ball, I would say, for forty-eight years. I have been employed by numerous ballclubs in the majors and in the minor leagues.

I entered in the minors with Kansas City. I played as low as Class D ball, which was at Shelbyville, Kentucky, and also Class C ball and Class A ball, and I have advanced in baseball as a ballplayer.

I had many years that I was not so successful as a ballplayer, as it is a game of skill. And then I was no doubt discharged by baseball in which I had to go back to the minor leagues as a manager, and after being in the minor leagues as a manager, I became a major league manager in several cities and was discharged . . . we call it discharged because there is no question I had to leave.

And I returned to the minor leagues at Milwaukee, Kansas City, and Oakland, California, and then returned to the major leagues. In the last ten years, naturally, with the New York Yankees, the Yankees have been a tremendous

success and while I am not a ballplayer who does the work
I have no doubt worked for a ballclub that is very capable
in the office.

I have been up and down the ladder. I know there are
some things in baseball thirty-five to fifty years ago that are
better now than they were in those days. In those days, my
goodness, you could not transfer a ballclub in the minor
leagues, Class D, Class C, Class A ball.

How could you transfer a ballclub when you did not
have a highway? How could you transfer a ballclub when
the railroads then would take you to a town, you got off,
and then you had to wait and sit up five hours to go to
another ballclub?

How could you run baseball then without night ball?
You had to have night ball to improve the proceeds, to pay
larger salaries, and I went to work, the first year I received
$135 a month. I thought that was amazing. I had to put
away enough money to go to dental college. I found out it
was not better in dentistry. I stayed in baseball.

KEFAUVER: Mr. Stengel, are you prepared to answer particularly
why baseball wants this bill passed?

STENGEL: Well, I would have to say at the present time, I
think that baseball has advanced in this respect for the
player help. That is an amazing statement for me to make,
because you can retire with an annuity at fifty and what
organization in America allows you to retire at fifty and
receive money?

Now the second thing about baseball that I think is
very interesting to the public or to all of us is that it is the
owner's fault if he does not improve his club, along with
the officials in the ballclub and the players.

Now what causes that? If I am going to go on the road
and we are a traveling ballclub and you know the cost of
transportation now—we travel sometimes with three
Pullman coaches, the New York Yankees on the road and
all—that it is the best, and we have broken records in

Washington this year, and we have broken them in every city but New York, and we have lost two clubs that have gone out of the city of New York.

Of course, we have had some bad weather. I would say that they are mad at us in Chicago, [but] we fill the parks. They have come out to see some good material. I will say they are mad at us in Kansas City, but we broke their attendance records.

Now, on the road we only get possibly twenty-seven cents. I am not positive of these figures, as I am not an official. If you go back fifteen years or if I owned stock in the club, I would give them to you.

KEFAUVER: Mr. Stengel, I am not sure that I made my questions clear.

STENGEL: Yes, sir. Well, that is all right. I am not sure I'm going to answer your questions perfectly, either.

I followed Casey after he had testified for forty-five minutes. When Senator Kefauver asked if I had any opinion on the antitrust amendment, I said, "My views are just about the same as Casey's."

The room sort of cracked up and they called a recess.

Stengel had been around so long that everywhere you turned you ran into someone who had either played for him or had been released or traded by him. Burdette was one and, to my surprise, Warren Spahn turned out to be another.

The '58 World Series opened in Milwaukee, with the two southpaws, Spahn and Ford, pairing off again. Spahn was a skinny, rookie left-hander in 1942 when the Boston Braves sent him back to one of their farm clubs after a brief stay.

The manager was Casey Stengel and the Braves were a last-place team, or close to it. Casey was hit by a taxi and broke a leg, missing several games, and in December the Press Club of Boston voted the cab driver their Man of the Year.

(Spahn did not return to the majors until after the war, in 1946. He would rejoin Stengel in 1965 with the Mets, another very bad club, in the double role of pitcher and coach. He was forty-four, struggling on the mound, and the rest of the staff complained that Spahnie only coached himself. There was a disagreement about how often he should pitch, and he was dropped at the All-Star break. "I played for Casey Stengel," said Spahn, "before and after he was a genius.")

Bill Skowron and Hank Bauer touched up Spahn for home runs and the Yankees held a 3-2 lead until the eighth. Then Eddie Mathews walked, Hank Aaron doubled, and Wes Covington's fly ball sent in the tying run.

We had killed a couple of rallies with our baserunning. Spahn picked Bauer off first base and Yogi was thrown out trying to go from first to third, or there might not have been extra innings. Later, we would hear wisecracks about the Yankees hiring detectives to follow us on the bases, not in the streets.

In the top of the tenth, Ryne Duren, who had relieved Ford, gave up three singles, the last by Bill Bruton knocking in the run that won the opener for the Braves, 4-3. Spahn went the distance and I was hitless with a walk in four trips.

Let me tell you about Spahn. Hitters would go into the clubhouse after taking what they called a "comfortable 0 for 4." They were not afraid to face him because he never seemed to overpower you. And he would get you on a line drive to an infielder, a ground ball, and two long flies. No pitcher ever knew better how to set up a hitter to hit the ball one inch from his true power.

Watching him from the dugout, Spahn's perfect pitching form impressed me even more. From the side, he seemed to be turning over, automatically, rhythmically, like one of those old riverboat wheels, with no strain on his arm. If a man from Mars dropped down beside him, he would have had no idea what Spahn was doing with that little round white thing, but he would have known at once that whatever he was doing, he did it better than anybody else.

More than any player I knew, Spahn considered himself immune to the attacks of time. He was then thirty-seven. He had pitched his first pro game in a place called Bradford in 1940. But his breaking pitches still dipped and wobbled like a tired moth. And he still had the rambling walk of a good high school athlete, sort of a duck walk, his shoulders swinging from side to side. He had done a job on us and now we had to face Burdette, who beat us three times a year ago.

Lew was opposed by Bob Turley, who had won twenty-one games for us during the regular season. Ace lefties the first day, ace righties the second.

I hit two homers off Burdette, just tomahawked them, but they had no effect on the outcome. The Braves scored seven runs in the first inning, starting with Bruton's leadoff homer and ending with a three-run clout by Burdette himself. Turley retired just one batter and took the loss, 13-5.

In the clubhouse after the game, a television interviewer stuck his microphone in Stengel's face and asked, "Do you think your team is choking?"

Casey growled at him, "Do you choke on that fucking microphone?" Then he turned his back to the camera and very deliberately scratched the seat of his pants. He gave me a wink as he walked by and said, "When I cursed, I knocked out their audio, and when I scratched my ass I ruined their picture."

It was a lousy flight home on our chartered United Airlines DC-7. I couldn't blame the Milwaukee fans, after last year's triumph, for feeling we were going to be easy pickings. We were headed to Yankee Stadium 0 and 2, and had lost with our two best pitchers. And Burdette was quoted in the next day's papers as saying he wished the Yankees were in the National League. "They would be lucky to finish fifth," he said.

Casey told the team and the press the same thing:

"We're not in what I would call a rosy position, but this thing is not over by a long shot. Why, only two years ago, we lost the first two to Brooklyn. I seem to remember that we won it at the end, didn't we? There's no law that says we can't do it again."

Don Larsen had a sore elbow but Stengel started him on one of his hunches. It paid off. We were desperate for a win and Larsen delivered. He gave us seven strong innings and Duren came in to finish the shutout, 4-0. Bauer accounted for all of the runs with a two-run single in the fifth and a two-run homer in the seventh.

That win picked us up big-time, but then Spahn came right back the next day and drove us into the ground like a railroad spike. He blanked us on two hits, 3-0, and his bloop single drove in one of the runs. I had a triple off the scoreboard with one out in the fourth, but Skowron tapped back to the mound and Schoendienst knocked down Berra's line drive, then threw him out. Hank Bauer had hit safely in seventeen straight games, but Spahn stopped it in Game 4. It was typical of Bauer's low profile that nobody seemed to realize he had a hitting streak until it was over.

Now, down three games to one, we were on our knees, and from my personal experience I can testify that is a painful position to be in.

The Braves sent out Burdette in Game 5 against Turley, and no one could accuse us of overconfidence. Lew had beaten us four in a row, and the jokes about his throwing the spitter were no longer funny. They had three games left to get one win, and the writers said the Braves were looking to Lew with great expectorations.

But as we say in Oklahoma, the sun don't shine on the same dog's ass every day. We finally broke out of our slump against the guy who had owned us, sending ten men to the plate in the sixth, scoring six times and going on to win, 7-0. The key hit was a two-run double by Gil McDougald, who opened the scoring with a homer in the third.

Bob Turley, who had gotten only one out in his last

start, was almost flawless this time. He put them down on five harmless singles. The Series was going to be decided at Milwaukee's County Stadium, and the Braves still led by one, with Spahn ready to go in Game 6. Stengel, who liked to spot Whitey's starts and sometimes skipped his turn, was sending him out on two days' rest.

The day was damp and misty in Milwaukee and the fans wore plaid lumberjackets and huddled under blankets. Rematches are tricky. This one didn't go according to plan, but it turned out fine. Bauer hit his fourth home run of the Series in the first inning, and the Milwaukee infielders kicked a ground ball in each of the first three, but we trailed, 2-1, after five.

Ford gave up two hits and a run in the first. He yielded three singles and a walk in the second, and with a run in and the bases loaded he was done. Casey waved in Art Ditmar. He had planned to go with Art and save Whitey for what he hoped would be the seventh game. Then he changed his mind. Now it was Ditmar, after all, who had to keep us in the Series.

With one out, Johnny Logan lifted a fly to Elston Howard in left and Andy Pafko came racing home after the catch. Yogi was waiting for him. Pafko dived for the plate and Berra slapped the ball against his skull—a double play and we were out of a potentially big, big inning.

In the sixth, I singled to right, went to third when Bruton fumbled Howard's hit and scored the tying run on Yogi's sacrifice fly. The game went into extra innings, still tied at 2-2, with Spahn now working his twenty-eighth inning. And like Ford, he had come back after two days of rest. McDougald led off the tenth with a homer and we finally got rid of Spahn with three singles, the last by Skowron producing the fourth run.

It was a cushion we were going to need. The Braves got one of the runs back on a run-scoring single by Aaron, and had the tying and winning runs on base when Turley came in to relieve Duren, who had given us four tough innings.

Turley got pinch hitter Frank Torre to pop up and the Series was dead even. We had come back from the grave.

The two pitchers who had started the seventh game last year, Larsen, the perfect stranger, and Burdette, the one-man army, were going to settle it. That seemed fitting. They were the two most heroic pitchers in recent World Series memory.

The Braves had blown two chances to put us away. Now they loaded the bases in the first inning with one out, filled them again with two out, and collected just one run. In the third, Casey yanked Larsen after he gave up two singles—in a short series, it's worth repeating, patience isn't a virtue.

The Braves filled the bases against Bob Turley with two out and got nothing. In between these wasted opportunities, Frank Torre made two throwing errors in the second inning and the Yankees scored twice, without a hit.

Burdette, who was using all the tools nature gave him, his arm and head and heart and tongue, gave his all for eight innings. But except for Del Crandall's game-tying homer in the sixth, he didn't get much help. He got the first two batters in the eighth, Berra doubled and scored the winning run on Howard's single. Carey singled off Mathews's glove and then the Moose added three more with a homer into the bleachers in left-center.

The four-run burst had made Turley the winner for the second time in three days, 6-2. In between, he had retired the last batter to save Game 6.

No team since Pittsburgh in 1925 had come back to win a World Series after trailing three games to one. So I would have to say that this was one of our sweetest. But honesty requires that I add, we won because Milwaukee wouldn't. They had it wrapped up but couldn't get the bundle home. The Braves didn't deserve to win, although Warren Spahn and Lew Burdette did. But, then, so did Turley. The World Championship was the eighteenth for the Yankees, and five out of seven since I had joined the club.

Still, I was a little envious of the Braves, who were still heroes to their fans. New Yorkers expected us to win. There had been no celebrations, no ticker-tape parades, and not much in the way of free beer and bratwurst.

No one could have foreseen, certainly not me, that the Braves would soon become what the fans will never toler- ate: a mediocre team, not good enough to win, not bad enough to be fun. The love affair would cool off and the franchise would move once again, this time to Atlanta, in 1965. Eddie Mathews would become the only player I knew who was a minor league hero in Milwaukee and Atlanta, and then returned to those cities years later, bringing the big leagues with him.

Not until the very end, when the city knew it was los- ing the team, did the fans in Milwaukee boo the Braves, and even then they spared Mathews.

It was that way on our club with Yogi, and I eventually figured out why. In 1958, when we both started slowly, they booed me, but not him. Even after I got hot they booed me, off and on, the rest of the season. It was partly because I struck out so much that year; and partly because no matter how well I did, they expected more. I think it all went back to that buildup before my rookie year. They wanted me to be Paul Bunyan and Ozark Ike and Jack Armstrong, the All-American boy. I wanted them to expect a lot. I didn't like the boos, but I knew that in a sense they were compliments, too.

They didn't expect less of Yogi, but he was the guy who made the Yankees seem almost human. The fans didn't really know him, of course. They only knew the surface stuff: the Yogi with the lovable, munchkin face, the Yogi whose words did a loop between the brain and the mouth. He helped you just by being in the batting order, or in the clubhouse.

There was nothing fake about him. He really enjoyed the simple pleasures. He had real fond memories of the Hotel Edison, where he lived as a bachelor in the late 1940s.

It was next door to the Copacabana, as I well knew, but that wasn't what Yogi remembered. "What a great place," he said. "My room cost me $4.50 a day. All the good movies were just around the corner, and nobody was afraid to go out at night."

There are a lot of places in a lot of cities that are not safe anymore and some of them are the streets and parking lots outside baseball stadiums.

But to know Yogi you had to see how kind and gentle and real he was.

Once, he agreed to speak at a father-and-son church banquet as a favor to a baseball writer from St. Louis. (That tells you something about Berra right there; he did favors for writers.)

Every son received a bat and ball and came up to have Yogi autograph them. At a corner table were some kids from a local orphanage. "Aren't they getting anything?" Yogi asked.

An organizer of the banquet told him that a couple of baseballs were being sent to the home for the orphans' use. "We think it's enough of a thrill for them just to be here," the man added.

Yogi got up from the head table, went to where the orphans were sitting, pulled up a chair, and began signing whatever the kids had. Someone at the head table finally said, "Yogi, we'd like you to come back up here and say a few words."

"Go on with the program," he sort of mumbled. "I'm busy. I'm talking to some of my friends." And he stayed there the rest of the evening.

# MAZ RETIRES CASEY

## 1960—PIRATES 4, YANKEES 3

The worst disappointment of my baseball career, and one that hurts to this day, was our loss to the Pittsburgh Pirates in the 1960 World Series. The better team lost, the only time I truly felt that way. It wasn't even close.

The Pirates last appeared in the Series in 1927, when the Yankees of Ruth and Gehrig swept them in four. What the hell, we had a reputation to maintain. We scored fifty-five runs, with ninety-one hits, twenty-seven for extra bases, and still lost. I had my most productive Series ever, batting .400, hitting three homers, driving in eleven runs, and scoring eight. I even had a big hit when we rallied to tie the score with two runs in the ninth inning of the final game. But we still lost.

Even now, thirty-four years later, I get upset when I think about it. The truth is, Casey blew it by not using Whitey Ford in the opener, which would have allowed him to start Whitey in three games. I didn't understand the decision then and I still don't.

There were undercurrents on that Yankee team that were not apparent to me until later. Maybe the back-room maneuvering caught up with us in October. Or maybe it was one of those moments when talent isn't enough. Sometimes it's better to be crazy or lucky or both.

But to understand whatever bridge the Yankees had crossed, you have to go back to the off-season after we lost the pennant in 1959. We had finished third, fifteen games behind the White Sox and ten games behind the second-place Indians.

In December, George Weiss swung a seven-player trade with the Kansas City A's. There was a standing gag around the league, that Kansas City had been a Yankee farm club for years—and it still was. We did make more than our share of one-sided deals with the A's, who had been sold and moved out of Philadelphia over the bitter objection of Connie Mack. The move came in the winter of 1955. The next winter Mr. Mack died.

So the reality was that the A's were a bad team in a small market and hurting for money. It wasn't hard for the Yankees to take advantage of them, although the news of this trade left the fans in New York less than thrilled.

We gave up Hank Bauer, whose first full season had been Casey's first, in 1949; Don Larsen, whose perfect game had assured him a permanent spot in Yankee legend; Norm Siebern, and Marv Throneberry. Marv turned up a few years later with the Mets, and earned much more fame as a symbol of their losing ways than he could possibly have known as a reserve with the Yankees.

In return, we acquired Joe DeMaestri, Kent Hadley, and Roger Maris. The first two wouldn't make an impression, but Maris made a lasting one, and I was among the few who had reason to think he might.

Roger had played the past two seasons at Kansas City under Harry Craft, my first manager in the minors. When our teams met, Harry and I would sometimes get together after the game for a drink at the hotel. I liked what I had seen of Maris, who had been a rookie with Cleveland in 1957, platooning in right field with Rocky Colavito. He had what we called line-drive power. You could string telephone wire on Roger's home runs. He didn't hit the high, soaring kind that seemed to parachute into the seats, like the Babe did and, yeah, like I did and later Reggie Jackson. One night, Harry Craft was just musing out loud, and he said if Roger was with the Yankees, aiming at that short fence in right field, 296 feet from home plate, he'd have a picnic. "He could be another Mickey Mantle," said Harry, grinning.

I was going to miss the players we gave up, especially Bauer, who had been my mentor during my early struggles in New York. Back then Jimmy Cannon had called me a bubblegum kid in a chewing tobacco league. He got that right.

But Roger Maris and I were going to have a special closeness, which probably seems easy for me to say, years after Roger's death. It is in the nature of people to look for the tension, the jealousy, maybe a feud between teammates. Those feelings may have been there with Ruth and Gehrig; according to the stories even their wives got into the act. It wasn't like that with Roger and me, but we kept it to ourselves. Our feeling was, let the press and the fans think what they wanted.

It didn't take long for Maris to be stamped as not being a New York kind of guy. He was a Fargo, North Dakota, kind of guy. Once, Bob Cerv and Roger had their wives fly in for a weekend, and the wives wanted to go sight-seeing. They even went to an art museum. I asked Roger how it was and he said, "They had a lot of old pictures in there."

When the trade was announced, Maris said he wasn't sure he wanted to leave Kansas City. He didn't think he would like New York. Of course, those sentiments made all the papers. Me, I was in awe of New York: the people, the noise, the traffic, the food, the night life. But I wanted to fit in. The veterans showed me the best places to eat and Bauer helped me upgrade my clothes. I taught myself how to overtip and overspend.

We were alike in a lot of ways. Both of us were recruited by the University of Oklahoma to play football. Roger, who once returned four kickoffs for touchdowns in a high school game, had a scholarship in his pocket. He took a bus halfway across the country, from Fargo to Oklahoma City. He should have stayed on for another couple of hours because the University is in Norman. He waited in Oklahoma City for two days, and when no one from the university showed up to meet him he got back on the bus and returned to Fargo. That's how he wound up playing pro baseball, instead of football.

When the 1960 season opened, I was batting in the second spot with Maris behind me. Casey was notorious for juggling his lineups, and in my career I had batted in each of the first five places in the order. Yogi would usually bat cleanup. By July I was hitting third, which I preferred, and Roger had moved to fourth. The order stayed that way for most of the season, but in October Casey switched us again. I was the clean-up man, behind Maris.

I found it hard to believe, but I was twenty-eight and in my tenth season with the Yankees. And for the first time in an injury-ridden career, I played what amounted to a full season, missing one game. I led the league in homers with 40, one more than Maris. He took the RBI title with 112, and we finished one-two in the voting for Most Valuable Player. Roger won by three votes. The balloting should not have been that close.

He had thirty-five homers by the first week in August and was ahead of Ruth's record pace *that* year. But he bruised his ribs trying to break up a double play, missed eighteen games and hit only four homers the rest of the way. I felt like dirt because I was the guy who hit into the double play. Even worse, I hadn't tried to run it out. I took a few steps and then stopped.

We were on our way to losing a doubleheader to the Senators and falling from first place to third. When the teams changed sides, Bob Cerv replaced me in center field.

Later, in the clubhouse, I had a fairly predictable dialogue with the writers: Had I reinjured myself running to first? No. Was I tired? No. Was my leaving the game Casey's idea? "Must have been. It wasn't mine."

It was bad enough losing twice, but Casey was furious with me, as he had every right to be. He gave the writers an earful, but then he softened the criticism. "He gets mad at himself," he said, "because he isn't hitting the ball good." I had not hit a homer in the first two weeks of August and had driven in a pair. I had to work up my nerve to explain what actually happened. I wasn't sulking or loafing. I just made a stupid mistake. The Washington dugout had been riding me hard. I started jawing back at them and got distracted. I thought the force at second had been the third out and the inning was over.

The single most significant change in the Yankees that year was in Stengel himself. I think age and the pressure—not to win, but to finish first every year—were catching up with him. He had gotten more cantankerous. He was drinking more. Some days when he came to the park with a hangover he would take a nap in the dugout during batting practice.

But the big change was in how he dealt with the younger players. He had been fairly flexible in the past. He needled rookies the same as he did the veterans, but with the kids there had been a softer edge. He used sarcasm to motivate you. But now what seemed like teasing came across as mean.

Everyone had a story to make whatever point they wanted to make. Jerry Lumpe was still a promising young second baseman when Casey said, "He looks like the greatest hitter in the world until you play him." Then there was

Bobby Richardson. "Look at him," said Casey. "He doesn't drink, he doesn't smoke, he doesn't stay out late, and he still can't hit .250."

See, Stengel was always looking for a second baseman with the grit and nerve of Billy Martin, but with more talent. He wanted the perfect second baseman, and there wasn't one. He was wrong though, about Richardson. Bobby had a good career and even hit .300 one year. But the old man wasn't wrong about much.

It used to puzzle the players that he always knew which ones were staying out late. When Rod Kanehl played for him with the Mets, he got a call one day to report to Stengel's office, where he was asked: "What kind of hours you keeping, Kanehl?"

"Good hours, Case."

"Good hours, my tit. You better start getting in on time."

Stengel never had bed checks, as many managers did, so Rod couldn't figure out how he knew who had been staying out late. I could have told him. Every time the Mets took an early-morning flight, the old man walked up and down the aisle. Anybody that was asleep before the plane left the ground would be called into his office for a talk. Good hours, my tit.

He could be cruel. He said Jimmy Piersall, who had returned to his career after a nervous breakdown, "can be great, but you got to play him in a cage." But later Piersall played for him with the Mets and Casey gave him nothing but praise.

He once went to the mound to relieve his starter, who had been pitching his way out of trouble the whole game. "I'm not tired," he complained. "Well, I'm tired of watching you," said Casey.

You never heard Stengel talk about "chemistry," a word that got real popular in sports during the 1980s. He didn't mind having a few odd ones around if they produced. One of our pitchers, Jim Coates, had a kind of sour disposition, and his nickname on the team was the Mummy because he slept with his eyes open. Edna Stengel was on one of our bus trips in 1959, and Coates was a few seats behind her, his eyes open, his head tilted at an angle. Edna happened to glance around the bus, then turned to Casey and said, "Dear, I think one of your players is dead."

When Bob Cerv was still a reserve outfielder, Casey sat down next to him on the bench before a game and whispered, "Nobody knows this, but one of us has just been traded to Kansas City." Three years later, he made a deal to bring Cerv back.

Talking about Stengel is a little like the blindfolded men who tried to describe a camel. He had a keen eye and an unfailing memory and a streak in him that was, well, tender. When Tony Kubek was a utility man and making around $7,000, Casey gave him a check for $25 as a small wedding gift, and told him to take his wife out to dinner. Kubek folded the check in a pocket and forgot about it. Then one Sunday morning in the winter, on his way to church in his hometown of Milwaukee, he realized he had no money for the collection box. He remembered the check, and he dashed into a drugstore and cashed it. The druggist was so pleased with the check, he wrote to Stengel and said he wanted to frame it and asked if he would mind if the check was never cashed. The thrifty Stengel replied, no, he would not.

In the spring, the first time he saw Kubek, Casey said, "You picked a funny place to take your wife to dinner."

There were days when he would be reflective, and he would regale the guys in the dugout with stories from his own playing career. Once he recalled a moment that had taken place in the 1930s when Casey was playing right field for the Pirates. That day a shiny new red fire engine was to be shown off at the ballpark. In honor of the occasion, a mock house had been erected of two-by-fours in center field. At the proper instant, the house was set afire and the fire engine was supposed to race onto the field and douse the flames.

"Only they forgot to measure the bull pen," recalled Casey. "The engine was too big. They couldn't drive it through the gate." So the house kept burning, finally tumbling upon itself. When it had burned to the ground, and still no fire engine, he could stand it no longer. "I filled a glass with water in the dugout," he said, "and I ran out like Charlie Chaplin and SHOOSH! I threw the water on the fire. It was almost out anyway. And you know something? The fire department was mad as hell at me."

Much is clearer to me now, years later, than it was at the time about my own relationship with Casey. He wanted me to be part of his legacy to the game. He wanted me to be the greatest player of all time, and he may have wanted that more than I wanted it for myself. Shoot, I wouldn't have minded if that had been the final judgment on my career. I don't want to use injuries as an excuse. When I was young and strong, I wasn't as dedicated as I needed to be. And by the time I was dedicated, my legs were gone.

When Casey wrote his autobiography and picked his all-time American League team, I wasn't on it. He included all the players he had seen between 1912 and 1960, and his center fielders were Ty Cobb, Joe DiMaggio, and Tris Speaker. The critics—baseball, book, whatever kind of critics there are—tried to make something of that. But I have no quarrel with Casey's choices. Cobb, DiMaggio, Speaker. He didn't pick those names out of a hat. He also said, "Mantle had more ability than any player I ever had" on his Yankee teams. I'm thankful for the years I had. They landed me in the Hall of Fame and Casey was a big part of them.

He was at heart a teacher. I didn't always give him the answers he wanted, but I never, ever, once tried to show him up or treat Casey with disrespect. I wasn't a rebel, but I had my own way of doing things. Right or wrong, I didn't always agree with his way.

There were hints all during the 1960 season that Stengel was under pressure to retire, and I probably should have been more aware of them. It might have been what he wanted, but Casey was the kind of man who resisted pressure.

I believe he might have stepped down on his own after the '59 season, but it gnawed at him too much, watching the White Sox and the Dodgers play in the World Series. For only the second time in my time with the Yankees, we were at home during the first week in October. I was unhappy about the year I had—.285, thirty-one homers, only seventy-five runs batted in. I had played most of July on a bad ankle and I felt a stabbing pain in my right shoulder whenever I swung and missed, batting left-handed.

I was even less happy when George Weiss sent me a contract for $55,000, a cut of more than 20 percent. I threatened to hold out, and we finally compromised on a $2,000 raise for 1960.

This was the stew of feelings I carried into the season, and I started badly. On Memorial Day, I was batting under .250 with six homers. After I caught a fly ball for the final out of a doubleheader, the fans climbed over the fence onto the field, and one of them punched me in the jaw. It caught me so completely by surprise I didn't have time to react. I was on soft foods for the next four days.

Every other power hitter on the club was off to a quick start: Yogi, Cerv, Skowron, Elston, and Maris, the new fellow, who was leading the league in homers and runs batted in.

Then came my bonehead play in August, when Roger was injured, and there was talk of my being benched, fined, and even suspended. The beat writers who covered the team kept asking Casey what he planned to do about me. I didn't know what to expect, really. I just knew I had to get my head straight and start helping the team. When I got to Yankee Stadium that night, a Monday, my name was on the lineup card. I didn't exactly take that as an act of faith. With Roger out, Casey needed my bat. The Orioles were in town, tied for first with the White Sox.

I never compared the nights when I was booed; it isn't quite the same as measuring home runs. But I believe that was about as loudly as I had been booed in my career. The fans really gave it to me, the moment I stuck my head out of the dugout and trotted out toward center field. I could hear the shouts clearly: "Run it, out, Mickey, run it out!"

The game turned into that popular scenario, where the boos turn to cheers. I hit a pair of two-run homers and we won, 4-3, behind the pitching of Art Ditmar. The victory moved us into first place, a half game ahead of Baltimore and Chicago. I did something rare for me, I tipped my cap to the crowd after each homer. Ted Williams didn't, and I thought maybe it looked like you were playing to the gallery. But this time I joked with the press: "I figured I better get on their good side while I could. The next time I strike out they'll be on me again."

But the truth was, I made the gesture out of sheer relief. I really needed a big game. A bad one, on top of what had happened the previous day, and my season could have been in the ashcan. When the writers surrounded Casey, he practically had a canary feather fluttering from his lip. "Now you ask me what I am going to do about Mantle," he said. "Well, I'm going to shake his hand. I am very appreciative."

We were on our way to a strong finish. I have two special memories of September. In Detroit, I hit a homer that cleared the right-field roof, left the park, and landed in a lumberyard. I now had three of the four homers ever hit out of Briggs Stadium; Ted Williams hit the first one in 1939. A couple of math whizzes did some calculating and figured that the ball traveled 643 feet in the air. That distance isn't chiseled in stone, but the homer is listed in the *Guinness Book of Sports Records,* along with the one in Washington.

Later in the month, Ty Cobb dropped by our locker room before the first game of a series with the Orioles. Stengel, who had played against him, called Cobb "superhuman. When he got that wild look in his eye, you knew this was the one bird nobody could beat." I don't recall what I said; I was just in awe. But Cobb went out of his way to greet me and offer advice. "Don't be upset when the fans boo you," he said. "That has happened to all of us. The good ones survive the booing."

That was a hot Yankee team that prepared to take on the Pirates. We finished the season with a 15-game winning streak and broke our own American League record for team homers with 193. I connected for my thirty-ninth and fortieth against the Senators, winning my fourth—and as it turned out, my final—home run crown. Both were off Chuck Stobbs, who had served up the original tape-measure shot in 1953.

I took Stobbs deep eight times in my career, and I can't blame him for getting tired of being asked about the one that left the park. "I gave up a homer to Joe DeMaestri once," he told a reporter, wearily, "and nobody ever asks me about that." I thought it was a pretty funny line.

I doubt that we ever felt more confident heading into a World Series. The season had been a complete turnaround, from seventy-nine wins and third place to ninety-seven wins and a pennant. We had the strongest infield I ever played with—Moose Skowron, Bobby Richardson, Tony Kubek, and Clete Boyer. I don't mean that we took the Pirates lightly. The oddsmakers rated us even, on the theory that the Yankee pitching had gotten spotty, while Pittsburgh had a solid staff that included Bob Friend, Vernon Law, and Harvey Haddix, with Elroy Face in the bull pen.

No one knew what was going through Stengel's mind; not that we usually did. But a writer asked him one of those typical writer's questions, would he quit if the Yankees lost the Series? And he replied, "Well, I made up my mind, but I made it up both ways."

Then Casey made the decision that would always puzzle me. He passed over Whitey Ford, our most proven winner, and started Art Ditmar in the opener at Forbes Field.

My own feeling was that the pitching staff suffered from the absence of Jim Turner. I don't know exactly what happened, but the management had been putting heat on Casey after the nosedive of '59. So Jim Turner was pushed out as pitching coach, and Eddie Lopat, who had been one of the club's aces in the early 1950s, replaced him. I never paid much notice to what went on with the brain trust, but I heard players on other teams say that Turner was the best pitching coach in the league.

Casey was partial to ground-ball pitchers, and he liked Ditmar because he threw a lot of low-breaking stuff. He was, in short, the type of pitcher Eddie Lopat had been. That may sound real basic, keeping the ball down instead of up; grounders lead to double plays. Jim Turner liked his pitchers to go with their best stuff. Different coaches had different theories.

Art Ditmar had won fifteen games and that was tops on the staff, which tells you we had gone through the season without a real ace. Our bull pen bailed us out, getting a big lift from Luis Arroyo, a left-hander picked up from Cincinnati. Whitey had missed some starts with tendonitis, and finished with twelve wins, but he was still our best, the pitcher the other guys believed in the most.

When Ditmar was announced as our starter for the opener, we were all buzzing about it. What about Whitey, who had won more World Series games than any pitcher in history? How could he not go with Whitey? But he did.

Before the game, Ditmar was asked which Pirate he feared the most and Artie answered, "Right now I fear all nine of 'em." As it turned out, he only had to fear Bill Virdon, Dick Groat, Bob Skinner, and Dick Stuart. By the time the others came to bat, Ditmar was gone. He only pitched to five men and retired one.

Three runs crossed in the first inning and the Pirates held on to win, 6-4. You sure couldn't tell from the final score how we pounded Vernon Law, who gave up ten hits in seven innings, and Elroy Face, who was touched for a pinch homer by Elston Howard in the ninth.

The top of our batting order, Kubek, Hector Lopez, and Maris, had three hits apiece. Unfortunately, our clean-up man went 0 for 3 and was called out twice on strikes. I had a sorry day and not much company; Richardson was the only other starter who failed to get at least one hit. But we would do our share of damage before the Series was over.

Having won their first pennant in thirty-three years, the Pirates had the whole town on fire. A judge postponed a murder trial on the grounds that a jury couldn't be expected to pay attention to the evidence with the World Series going on.

So this was no small deal in Pittsburgh, one of the first cities to be rebuilt under the Urban Renewal Act. This was a national showcase for the new Pittsburgh, with its broad green plazas and dancing water fountains and modern skyscrapers. It was a shock to anyone who remembered the grimy old eyesores of the area downtown, where the three rivers were joined. The old buildings had been covered with years of soot. Now it was called, with some fitness, the Golden Triangle.

I looked at the Pirates and saw a club that had a bunch of battlers: Dick Groat, who led the National League in hitting, Smoky Burgess, and Don Hoak. At twenty-six, Roberto Clemente was already one of the most consistent players in the game, a .300 hitter with power, speed, and a great arm. Dick Stuart was a free swinger, kind of clumsy at first base, and fun to watch.

Bill Mazeroski made their infield click, and Bill Virdon in center was the most underrated outfielder in the game. The managers and coaches voted in a newspaper poll in the 1960s on whether Mays or Snider was the National League's best center fielder. The winner was Virdon.

He took us out of a big inning in the fourth, when Berra drove one to the deepest point in right-center, 425 feet from home plate, with two on and nobody out. Virdon climbed the wall with Clemente almost on his back and made the catch, spiking Roberto slightly on the leg on the way down. That one probably ranks among the half dozen most difficult World Series catches, but it was lost in the dizzy stuff that was still to come.

Of course, everything is magnified in a best-of-seven series, and the winner's share might be a third higher than the loser's. Back then, that was the way they split the pay-off. Trailing 3-1, Stengel sent up Dale Long to pinch-hit for Clete Boyer in the *second* inning. Clete's family was there to see him play, including his brother Ken, a great third baseman for the Cardinals. I'm not sure Clete ever got over being lifted before his first time at bat in the World Series.

But Casey figured that scoring chances were going to be scarce against Vernon Law, known as The Deacon, a twenty-game winner for the Pirates. Law was an ordained minister in the Church of Jesus Christ of the Latter Day Saints, and he was qualified to perform marriages, baptize babies, and tuck a pretty fair fastball under your chin. He gave a tithe to his church, I heard it was ten percent of what he made, so I guess this may have been the first time the Mormons had a direct financial interest in how the World Series came out.

It rained Wednesday night and Thursday morning, and again just before game time. The Pirates must have wished it had never stopped. In the pitching matchup they sent Bob Friend, their second-biggest gun, with eighteen wins, against Bob Turley (9-3). This game set the pattern: the Yankees winning by big margins and the Pirates taking the tight ones. Both managers, Stengel and Danny Murtaugh, were going quickly to their bull pens. Friend was lifted after four innings, down 3-0, and we pounced on five relief pitchers for nineteen hits and a 16-3 cakewalk.

We put it away with seven runs in the sixth, as twelve men batted. Elston Howard had a triple and a single in the same inning, and Bobby Richardson had a double and a single.

I was still having trouble trying to bat from the left side and struck out the first time I faced Friend. I was like a lab rat. I knew the pain was coming and I couldn't pull the trigger. I was hitless in my last ten at bats in the World Series, dating back to Game 6 in 1958. Then the Pirates brought in a couple of southpaws and I was able to turn around. I homered twice from the right side, driving in five runs and tying a Series record held by Tony Lazzeri, Bill Dickey, and Ted Kluszewski. The second homer cleared the wall at the 435-foot sign in center, where no right-handed hitter had ever before hit a ball. It had been done three other times by left-handed swingers Stan Musial, Duke Snider, and Dale Long, an ex-Pirate who was now on our bench.

In the ninth, the Pirates scored twice and Stengel called in Bobby Shantz, the glory tot of the old Philadelphia A's, to protect the lead. That was kind of funny when you think about it, taking out Turley when he was ahead, 16-3. I kidded Casey about getting conservative ever since he bought a bank—I heard it was Edna's money—in Glendale, California, where they lived. It seemed true, though. He was seventy and rich, and he had gotten more conservative. And the bank was doing so well, he said, that even two sportswriters had accounts there—"fifteen or twenty dollars," he said, "their life savings."

We were going back to New York with the Series tied, and the Pirates were far from depressed. "Anybody get hurt out there today?" asked Murtaugh, when they straggled into the clubhouse. "No? Then we're okay."

Over in our place, a photographer asked Stengel to look happy. "Hooray for us," he said.

Whatever the reason, Casey had saved Whitey Ford for our home opener in Yankee Stadium and he was at the top of his form with a four-hit shutout. He just went about his business like a butcher cleaning his Christmas turkey. We made it fairly easy for him, scoring six runs in the first inning, including a grand-slam homer by Bobby Richardson. The score was 10-0.

I had four hits, including my fourteenth homer, leaving me one behind Babe Ruth in World Series play. But the record I had tied two days earlier, for driving in runs in a single game, fell to Richardson, another example of how the Series is so unpredictable, and such a stage for the unlikely hero.

Clem Labine, the ex-Dodger, was pitching when Bobby popped his homer into the left-field seats. In the past two seasons, he had produced a total of three home runs—two in 1959 and one in 1960. George Witt was on the mound when he drove in two more runs with a bases-loaded single in the fourth inning. That gave him a total of six and the new record. He had knocked in twenty-six during the regular season, a total of seven since the All-Star Game.

But here in the biggest spectacle in baseball, he had done something, as Red Smith pointed out, "never accomplished by Babe Ruth, Rogers Hornsby, Mr. Muscles Mantle, or Paul Bunyan's Blue Ox Babe." Bobby described himself as "dad-gummed surprised," and seemed almost embarrassed by his performance. He was twenty-five that year, a native of Sumter, South Carolina, where in the off-season he ran the YMCA. "Dad-gum" was about as rough as his language ever got.

The paid attendance at Yankee Stadium was 70,001, and sitting in the VIP seats were former president Herbert Hoover and Prime Minister Nehru of India. Not many years later, Nehru's jackets, cut straight with a high collar, caught on in the United States in men's fashions. I bought one, but I got lucky and don't believe I was ever photographed in it.

Hoover, who was in his eighties, received a nice ovation from the crowd. I understood he had been booed without mercy when he appeared at the ballpark in 1931, when he was president during the Depression.

The Pirates went back to their first-game formula to even the Series, Vernon Law starting—against Ralph Terry—

Elroy Face coming to his aid, and Bill Virdon turning in the defensive gem. They beat us, 3-2, with Law getting two hits, one a run-scoring double. Moose Skowron had broken a scoreless tie in the fourth with a solo homer, but the middle of our batting order—Maris, me, and Berra—went hitless.

The tying and winning runs were on base with one out in the seventh when Face, not a very intimidating figure at five-eight and 155 pounds, was waved in to face big, burly Bob Cerv. On a 1-1 pitch, Cerv crunched one and sent it on a towering arc toward the bleachers in right-center. But there was Virdon racing with his back to the plate. He made a leaping catch, bounced off the wall, and tumbled to the ground. He raised his glove to show he still had the ball.

Face retired eight straight batters to hold the lead, but Virdon had already made the game-saving catch. You know when you have made one, no matter what the score or the inning, and I can tell you that it feels really fine.

The Pirates trotted out their little left-hander, Harvey Haddix, for Game 5, and we countered with Art Ditmar, the loser in the opener. Haddix was about the same size as Face, an Ohio farmer with a lean face and spindly build. He broke in with the Cardinals after the war, and since they already had a pitcher similar in style and looks named Harry "The Cat" Brecheen, Harvey Haddix became "The Kitten." It fit him. He pitched for the Phillies and the Reds before he found his fame in Pittsburgh. He won twenty games one year, and he did what no pitcher in the history of the game had ever done: he pitched twelve perfect innings, thirty-six up and thirty-six down, and lost the game to the Milwaukee Braves in the thirteenth, 1-0.

If you tend to overswing, you hate to face a pitcher like Haddix, who can twist you into a pretzel. Bob Friend was rested and the reporters were calling the decision a gamble. We knew the Pirates didn't feel that way. "What the hell are you talkin' about?" said Don Hoak, whirling around when a writer put it to a question. "That little [bleep] has a heart as big as a [bleepin'] barrel."

We worried a run out of him in the second on a hit and two ground balls, and another in the third when Maris homered into the upper deck in right field. That was it. Ditmar didn't make it through the second inning, as the Pirates scored three runs on three hits—two of them doubles—and an error. Again, Face entered the game in the seventh with the tying runs aboard, and got the last eight outs in a 5-2 victory. I was the only Yankee to reach base against Face, on a walk. They took me out of the game, these two terrific pests, with three walks and a strikeout. Haddix held us to five hits and no Yankee had more than one. David was spitting in Goliath's face.

When we clobbered the Pirates, 16-3 and 10-0, to go up two games to one, everybody thought it was time to concentrate on the football season. Instead, we were going back to Pittsburgh, needing to win two straight. The last time we had played in the World Series, in 1958, we had to finish three-for-three, and we did.

For the second time in five days, Whitey Ford pitched a shutout and the Yankees crushed the Pirates, 12-0, lashing seventeen hits off six pitchers, starting with Bob Friend. The numbers were gruesome. Each team now had three wins, ours by a margin of thirty-five runs, theirs by six. We had already produced more hits (78) and runs (46) than any other World Series team ever did, and we broke the records going back to the days when they played best five of nine.

Maris, Berra, and John Blanchard had three hits each. Yogi was in left field, and Blanchard was subbing behind the plate for Elston Howard, who turned up with a broken hand. The Pirates couldn't compare with our bench strength or balance. Three of us—me, Yogi, and even Whitey—drove in two runs. Richardson tripled twice and knocked in three more.

So how come those jokers were still hanging around? Why hadn't the Yankees wrapped it up and gone fishing? The answer was that Vernon Law started two games for Pittsburgh and Elroy Face relieved in three. But this day the Bucs were Lawless and Faceless. By the third inning they were also Friendless.

There never had been a Series as wacky as this one. It also left Casey's decision to hold back Ford even more open to second-guessing. And with leads of ten and twelve runs, he let Whitey pitch complete games, eliminating the chance that he might have been available for a batter or two in relief in the seventh game. As it turned out, we could have used him.

You wonder what a manager tells a team that has been blown out as badly as the Pirates. Danny Murtaugh had a classic Irish mug and a tough Irish hide, and what he told them was: "I looked in the rule book and it said the Series will be decided on games won, not on runs scored."

I wish it had been the other way.

There were all kinds of rumors during the week about Stengel retiring, not retiring, being forced out. Before we took the field for the final game, Casey told the team: "Win or lose, this has been a good year and I want to thank you for everything." That sounded a little like a farewell speech.

Game 7 had a storybook ending—for them. Vernon Law made his third start, with Bob Turley going for us. Rocky Nelson touched Turley for a two-run homer in the first and a leadoff single to Smoky Burgess in the second and he was gone. Bill Stafford got out of the inning after two runs had scored and we were already down, 4-0.

Bobby Shantz gave us a chance to climb back in the game, stopping them for five innings on one single. A homer by Skowron in the fifth cut the score to 4-1. An inning later, two men reached base and Face ambled out of the bull pen to relieve Law. For the first time in the Series, Elroy struggled. I singled in a run and Yogi followed with a three-run homer into the upper deck in right, barely fair.

That rally put us ahead, 5-4, and with Shantz almost perfect in relief the props were in place for a sentimental ending.

I mean, if this was going to be Casey's last game, it was
fitting that the big blow would be delivered by Yogi, the
only Yankee who was there when Stengel arrived in New
York in 1949. We pushed across two more runs in the top
of the eighth off Face, and hiked the lead to 7-4. Looking
good.

In the bottom of the inning, the Pirates erupted for five
runs and it all started with a pebble. Gino Cimoli led off
with a pinch single and then Bill Virdon bounced a double-
play ball toward Tony Kubek at short. Just as Tony moved in
the ball hit the pebble, took a crazy bounce, and caught him
in the throat. He went down, and both runners were safe.
No pebble, no bad hop. We get the double play and Shantz
probably pitches out of the inning. Kubek had a swollen
windpipe, and he couldn't tell the trainer he wanted to stay
in the game. Poor Tony. He was Rookie of the Year at twenty, played short, third, and all three outfield positions, and
had nine good years. But most fans remember him for an
incident that took ten seconds, getting hit in the throat by
a freak bounce of the ball. He was in the hospital when the
game ended, two or three dramatic shifts later.

DeMaestri replaced Kubek at short. A hit and a run later,
Jim Coates replaced Shantz. Another single, a sacrifice bunt,
and an infield hit by Clemente let in another run and the
score was 7-6. There were two on and two out and the batter was Hal Smith, their back-up catcher. There were actually two catchers named Hal Smith in the National League.
The Hal Smith who was with St. Louis had a promising
career cut short by a balky heart. This was the other one.

On a 2-2 pitch, Smith rifled a three-run homer over the
ivied wall of brick in left field and the Pirates led, 9-7. As
Coates watched the ball vanish, he flung his glove high in
the air. Before the glove came down, Stengel was on his

way to the mound to bring in Ralph Terry, who got Don Hoak on a fly ball to retire the side.

Fortune turned a false smile on us in the top of the ninth. Bob Friend was on the mound and Richardson led off with a single. Dale Long pinch-hit for DeMaestri and singled. Now Haddix replaced Friend and got Maris on a pop-up to the catcher. I singled to drive in Richardson and the tying run scored on Berra's grounder to first. The game had slipped out of their hands, then ours, then theirs and now it was tied, 9-all.

The game stayed tied until the first batter in the bottom of the ninth, who happened to be Bill Mazeroski, tagged Ralph Terry's second pitch, a high slider, for a game-ending, Series-winning home run over the left-field wall. I'm sure not taking anything away from Maz, but that was a tough spot for Terry. He had warmed up five different times in the bull pen. I can still see Terry trying to weave his way through the fans who were running onto the field. I can still see Mazeroski being swallowed up by his teammates as he crossed home plate.

The Yankees walked off the field like zombies, and I'm not embarrassed to say I cried in the clubhouse. I was angry at Casey all over again for getting cute with the way he used Whitey. I loved Casey, I really did. He was a big part of my career. But I believe he blew that one.

On the plane ride home to Dallas, I was still puddling up and Merlyn tried to console me. She finally said, "Mickey, it's only a game." She meant well, but it didn't help. Just then, except for someone close to me dying, I felt as bad as I had ever felt in my life.

I realize that may sound like my priorities were screwed up, and maybe they were. The presidential election was less than a month away, and one of the 1960 Kennedy-Nixon debates had been held the night of one of our World Series games. The only time I paid any attention to politics was when Kennedy went to the All-Star Game in July, and met

Stan Musial, who was nearing the end of his career. They shook hands and Kennedy, the same age as Stan, smiled and said, "They tell me you're too old to run at forty-two, and I'm too young."

The question of age came up again five days after the Series ended. The loss gave the management of the Yankees the opportunity they needed to ease Stengel out and promote Ralph Houk. It would have been awkward to retire Casey if we had won, and the club wanted it to appear that the decision was his. They felt some pressure to move because Ralph had been approached about the Kansas City job.

The Yankees had secretly signed Houk to a contract and now they hoped that Casey would go quietly. They called a press conference on Tuesday at the Savoy Hilton in New York to announce his retirement. But when Casey went to the microphone, the New York writers asked if he had been fired. He looked testy, and he snapped, "Write anything you want. Quit, fired, whatever you please. I don't care."

But later, he said, "I was told my services were no longer required. I know this. I'll never make the mistake of being seventy again." Casey wanted it to be his choice and it wasn't. Like a lot of great actors, he knew it was time to leave the stage and he couldn't.

The Yankees held another press conference Friday and introduced Ralph Houk as the new manager. I felt sad for Casey, but I was excited that Houk would be his successor. He was forty-one and had been with the Yankees for eighteen seasons. He spent most of his playing days behind Berra, as a second- and-third string catcher. He could have been a starter for a lot of teams. He had managed Denver for three seasons and helped develop several of the players on our roster. He had coached at first base and in the bull pen and I don't know anyone who didn't respect him. He had been decorated during the war, saw a lot of action, and we called him "The Major." I called Ralph right away to say how glad I was for him—and the Yankees and myself.

When I flew to New York in mid-January to sign my new contract, the writers tried to get me to say something critical or controversial. I had gotten pretty good at deflecting their questions. How would a rookie manager like Houk do with a club as experienced as the Yankees?

"A manager who has the respect of his players can win," I said, "and Ralph has it."

Didn't Casey have the respect of his players?

"Sure," I said, "Casey had it, too."

Didn't you and Casey have differences?

I couldn't hold back a grin on that one. "Only those that were printed," I said.

Someone mentioned the criticisms Casey had aimed at me.

"Whatever Casey said about me was right," I replied, and I meant it.

I sure couldn't resent Stengel for wanting me to be great. I was leaving the room when Ralph started taking questions. One of the first had to do with expansion of the American League and if my legs would hold up through the longer, 162-game schedule.

In an offhanded way, he made a comment that was almost eerie. "I hope he plays a hundred and sixty-two games," he said, "and if he hits sixty homers and Maris hits fifty-nine they'll make me a helluva manager."

My game-winning homer put that smile on Merlyn's face as we leave Yankee Stadium in April 1965. (*National Baseball Library and Archives, Cooperstown, NY*)

The Mantles take a holiday trip to Joplin, Missouri. I think I see some family resemblance. That's Danny, Mickey Jr., Billy, and David in between Mom and Dad. (*National Baseball Library and Archives, Cooperstown, NY*)

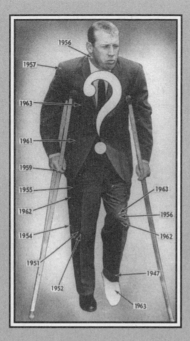

1956
1957
1963
1961
1959
1955
1962
1954
1951
1952

1963
1956
1962
1947
1963

I'm a walking poster boy for the orthopedic industry. Count 'em—fifteen fractures, injuries, or surgeries. (*National Baseball Library and Archives, Cooperstown, NY*)

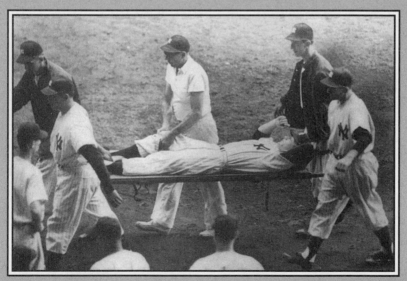

Not the way you want to leave the field. This injury in Game 2 of the '51 Series haunted my whole career. (*Photo by Jack Frank; National Baseball Library and Archives, Cooperstown, NY*)

**Looks like spring training and I'm being overcoached by Yogi, Joe D., and Ralph Houk. (*National Baseball Library and Archives, Cooperstown, NY*)**

**When Joe DiMaggio showed up for an old-timers game, he never seemed to age or gain an ounce. There was Joe, and then there were all the other center fielders who ever played the game. (*National Baseball Library and Archives, Cooperstown, NY*)**

I should have known we were in trouble. Whitey Ford is trying to give me a batting tip before we face the Pirates in 1960, the World Series I most hated to lose. (*National Baseball Library and Archives, Cooperstown, NY*)

Those were the go-go days. I was retired in 1970 when I teamed up with Joe Namath, the Jets' quarterback, to form an employment agency called "Mantle Men and Namath Girls." Joe got the girls, but the job market couldn't keep us in business. (*National Baseball Library and Archives, Cooperstown, NY*)

One of the rare photographs ever taken when Casey Stengel wasn't mugging for the camera. (*National Baseball Library and Archives, Cooperstown, NY*)

Casey Stengel (37) introduces me and my teammates to his close personal friend, Ike Eisenhower, before the start of the 1956 World Series at Ebbets Field in Brooklyn. (*National Baseball Library and Archives, Cooperstown, NY*)

Yogi led the reception after my only Series grand slam helped beat Brooklyn in Game 5 in 1953. That's Hank Bauer and Joe Collins waiting to shake my hand. We didn't need high fives in those days. (*National Baseball Library and Archives, Cooperstown, NY*)

In the '62 series, Willie Mays and I didn't live up to our billing. He played longer, and his career numbers were better than mine, but I beat him on the golf course. (*National Baseball Library and Archives, Cooperstown, NY*)

My ninth-inning homer made Jim Bouton the winning pitcher over the Cardinals in the third game of the '64 classic. Bouton wasn't always as popular in the Yankee clubhouse as he was that day. That photo hangs on the wall in my trophy room. (*National Baseball Library and Archives, Cooperstown, NY*)

I found a quiet moment and a quiet spot to read my fan mail as a rookie in 1951. I had the most loyal fans in the world. If I said something nice about Willie Mays or Duke Snider, they would write and argue with me. (*National Baseball Library and Archives, Cooperstown, NY*)

Time plays funny tricks. As a schoolboy, my dad took me to see Stan Musial play in the minors. Now we were friendly rivals in the 1960 All-Star Game at Yankee Stadium. (*National Baseball Library and Archives, Cooperstown, NY*)

This home run beat the Orioles in our opening game in 1962. Sometimes that memory comes back to me so strong—the feeling in my hands as the ball flies off the bat—and I really miss it. (*National Baseball Library and Archives, Cooperstown, NY*)

In '52, long-distance calls from the Big Apple to Commerce, Oklahoma, still impressed my mom. *(Copyright © 1993 New York Yankees)*

When I came home in 1952, I was treated like a hero. The small type in the sign in the window says, "A COUNTRY BOY WHO MADE GOOD IN THE BIG CITY." Ben Epstein, the famous New York writer, is on the right. That's our druggist, Ott Chandler, with his arm around me. *(Copyright © 1993 New York Yankees)*

In the early fifties, I still worked in the off-season in the mines, alongside my dad, Mutt Mantle (left), and Cliff Mapes, who played briefly with the Yankees. *(Copyright © 1993 New York Yankees)*

My twin brothers, Roy and Ray, might have made it as pros in baseball or football, but they didn't get the breaks I did. *(Copyright © 1993 New York Yankees)*

There was a certain fitness to Whitey and Mickey going into the Hall of Fame in the same class in 1974. It was worth at least a hug. *(Copyright © 1993 New York Yankees)*

I had one of my biggest games, two homers and five runs batted in, to help make Bob Turley an easy 16-3 winner over the Pirates in 1960. *(Copyright © 1993 New York Yankees)*

It was an honor for Roger Maris and me to be interviewed by the legendary broadcaster Red Barber in that special year, 1961. *(Copyright © 1993 New York Yankees)*

**When I swung the bat, I put everything into it, including my teeth.**
*(Copyright © 1993 New York Yankees)*

I'm a most happy fella as Billy Martin congratulates me on winning the Most Valuable Player award for the 1956 season. *(Courtesy* Houston Post)

I guess the uniforms were blank because no team would claim us. Phil Rizzuto (left) and Whitey Ford helped me produce a videotape, *Baseball Tips for Kids for All Ages.* *(Copyright © 1986 Mickey Mantle Sports Productions, Inc.)*

I returned to the Astrodome in 1985 to celebrate the twentieth anniversary of the opening of the world's first covered stadium. I hit the first indoor home run.

Billy Martin and I share a laugh in Fort Lauderdale in 1978. That western hat didn't qualify Billy as a cowboy. But then, nothing would.

I enjoyed having Yogi Berra as a manager, but I missed batting behind him, or even in front of him. (*Courtesy* Houston Post)

We were all smiling in spring training in 1966, but Johnny Keane (left) wouldn't finish the season as manager. I didn't have much reason to be happy either, nor did Ralph Houk. (*Courtesy* Houston Post)

When I signed my next-to-last Yankee contract in 1967, Ralph Houk had plans to convert me into a first baseman. But I kept my outfielder's glove for security. (*Courtesy* Houston Post)

I went to Florida in 1981 to help the Yankees as a batting coach in spring training. Billy Martin told me that if he needed to show somebody how to strike out, he'd call me.

# THE M&M BOYS

## 1961—YANKEES 4, REDLEGS 1

The Pirates had waited thirty-three years to return to the World Series. The Reds had been spotted in one as recently as 1940. Milwaukee wasn't even in the big leagues when the Yankees began our run, in '49, of playing in nine out of ten. Teams were rising from the tombs to take us on.

The stars of the 1961 World Series were not named Maris or Mantle. Their names were Skowron, Richardson, Blanchard, and Ford. A little-known relief pitcher, Bud Daley, acquired by the Yankees in June, blanked the Reds the last six and two-thirds innings to close out the Series in five games.

But how we got there—the race within the race—was the great Ghost Story of baseball's exploding summer. No one could have predicted a season so loaded with controversy or commotion or an irony so thick you could choke on it.

You would have thought that going from Casey Stengel to Ralph Houk required an adjustment so great, the Yankees in 1961 would need counseling more than spring training. But it wasn't that tough. Everyone knew there was only one Casey, and he was a complicated piece of work. I missed the sight of him, the walk like Popeye the Sailor, with legs so lumpy it looked as though he were smuggling walnuts in his stockings. He even made umpires laugh.

Ralph wasn't colorful and he wasn't complicated. He was strong as pig iron, firm, direct, sure of himself, a straight shooter. Casey liked Houk and was able to kid around with him. As the bull pen coach, one of the Major's lesser duties was to guard the ball bag, which contained the new baseballs for that day's game. Before one of our World Series openers, Ralph left it for a moment next to the dugout and when he turned around it was gone. A kid had leaned over a rail, grabbed it, and run.

Casey just shook his hand. "How can you capture all them Germans," he asked, "and not be able to guard a ball bag?"

Stengel dropped hints that Houk was his personal choice to replace him. I think he felt that way when he said it, but I don't care what business you are in, from what I've seen great men just don't want to be replaced, ever.

So there was resentment on Casey's part about the way the Yankees let him go, and some of it rubbed off on Ralph. When you add it up—the history of the Yankees, succeeding a manager who had won ten pennants and was, on top of it, the best showman baseball had ever known—the pressure on Houk had to be like having an elephant sitting on your chest.

He lost part of his bench in the expansion draft, and the Yankees were changing. Yogi was no longer an everyday catcher. The pitching staff needed an overhaul. Yet, in spite of how uncertain we looked in the spring, I wasn't surprised that we made it back to the World Series and trounced Cincinnati. What surprised me was that our season came together in such a way as to make the '61 Series almost an anticlimax. I say "almost" because if you lose, the records and the awards feel tainted. Losing puts a major dent in the trip that got you there.

I didn't need to be sold on Ralph Houk, but one of his first acts was to urge me to step up and become the leader of the team. Houk didn't flatter people and he didn't play mind games. So I had no reason to feel he was conning me when he said I was the obvious guy, the player the others looked to, the big man on the club. Those are not terms that I use lightly. I had just never thought about it. When you get treated like a kid for so long, you don't outgrow it right away. After a while, you may not want to outgrow it.

I had been so raw when I joined the club in 1951, I never saw myself in that role, not as long as the Yankees had a DiMaggio or Bauer or Berra, or the veteran pitchers, Reynolds, Raschi, or Lopat. My main handicap was just being young, which is curable. What made it work for me was the fact that I wasn't self-appointed. Houk talked it up to the press. I was going to be the team leader because he kept saying so; as Mantle goes, so go the Yankees.

He also told me he planned on leaving me in the clean-up spot. I really preferred batting third, but he convinced me it would be better for the team. And it was. It made a better hitter out of Roger without hurting me any. Most of all, I felt a sense of responsibility. Ralph was depending on me.

It isn't easy and it isn't wise to pick out one season or another as the most suspenseful, the most exciting, the most turbulent. But it seems to me that years ending in "one" tend to be special. In 1941, Joe DiMaggio hit safely in fifty-six straight games. In 1951 Bobby Thomson's home run off Ralph Branca lifted the New York Giants past the Brooklyn Dodgers in a playoff to decide the most historic of all pennant races.

And in 1961, Roger Maris hit sixty-one home runs to break Babe Ruth's record for most in a season, set in 1927, the year Lindbergh flew alone across the Atlantic. I finished with fifty-four, as the two of us chased the Babe's ghost all summer, and the Yankees went sailing into the World Series like Slim Pickens riding the guided missile in the movie *Dr. Strangelove.*

Houk had a plan and he wasted no time putting it in place. He wasn't the kind of guy who needed all day to look at a horseshoe. He hired Johnny Sain, who had finished his career with the Yankees, as his pitching coach. Sain's peak years were with the Braves, when the fans had a slogan: "Spahn and Sain and pray for rain."

He made Yogi his regular left fielder, making room behind the plate for Howard and Blanchard. I was the designated team leader and he showed his confidence in me by telling not only the players, but the writers. He wanted people to know that this wasn't some kind of symbolic role, where I would take the lineup card to the umpires.

More important, he wanted me to know. In doing this, he made me a better player and perhaps a better person. When I was bothered by an injury or playing poorly, I tended to be withdrawn. Some of this was just self-protection. But you can't lead a team by sulking.

Another element of Ralph's plan was to convert Ryne Duren into a starter. He had appeared in forty or more games in relief in each of the last three seasons. Two years earlier, he had an earned run average of 1.88. Duren may have been the first relief pitcher to rely almost entirely on his fastball. Hitters feared him, partly because he seldom knew where the ball was going. Sometimes he turned his wildness into an advantage. He wore thick glasses and his eyes were so bad he wore them when he took a shower, I guess so he could find the soap.

When he came in from the bull pen he would throw his first pitch over the catcher's head. This tended to discourage hitters from digging in on him.

Once, Duren walked three straight batters on twelve pitches, forcing in a run. He stormed up to the plate umpire and demanded to know, "Where the [bleep] are those pitches?"

The umpire raised his hand to his chin. "Well, dammit," fumed Ryne, "I've got to have that pitch." Meaning that he considered it close enough to be called a strike. When we finally got out of the inning, the guys on the bench buried their heads in their shirtsleeve, trying not to laugh.

But Ralph shelved the idea of turning him into a starter because Duren had a drinking problem. I don't think he ever showed up at the ballpark loaded, but there were several times that spring where he got noisy and unruly and made a scene. Houk had to discipline him because the whole team knew what was going on. Ryne was slapped with a fairly stiff fine, but the results were short term. "After I fined him," said Ralph, "I imagine he didn't drink again for, oh, maybe four or five hours." Sober, he was as nice a fellow as you could ever hope to meet. No one wanted him to find himself more than Houk. He had been Duren's manager in Denver and urged Stengel to bring him to New York.

He wasn't a mean or destructive drunk, but Duren would get what Casey called "whiskey slick." On the train coming home after we had won the 1958 pennant, Ryne spotted Ralph after dinner, about to light a cigar, anticipating that first soothing puff. And he walked over and playfully mashed the cigar all over Houk's face. There wasn't going to be any fight. Duren knew all about Houk's war record and his toughness. Ralph didn't hit him, but he stood and pushed him away, sort of swatting Ryne across the side of his head. Unfortunately, Ralph was wearing one of his heavy, diamond-encrusted World Series rings. It opened a cut above Ryne's eye, and he wandered through the cars almost in tears, pointing to the cut and asking if this was any way to treat a friend? The story got a lot of play. In the *New York Post*, Leonard Schecter said the ring left a hole big enough to stick a martini onion in it.

The heavy drinking cut short Duren's career and broke up his first marriage. "You'll keep the devil if he can win for you," said Houk, and the thing was, he liked Ryne. We all did. But three weeks into the season, the Yankees traded him to the Angels.

Duren was with the Senators when he threw his last pitches. At one point Gil Hodges, their manager, had to talk him down from a bridge. Later, he stopped drinking, cleaned up his life, and began to counsel people who were drug or alcohol abusers. He once said that he could look back at a photo of his old Yankee teams and spot thirteen alcoholics.

In March of '61, there wasn't much World Series talk. There was more concern about whether we could just survive spring training. We lost eight of our first nine games and Luis Arroyo was hit on his left arm, his pitching arm, by a line drive and suffered a hairline fracture. There went half the bull pen.

Every writer who visited our camp had to do the comparison story, Stengel and Houk, at least once. I was busting my tail, in the best shape I had been in since my rookie year, trying to get the club untracked and justify Ralph's faith in me. I wondered if he needed any cheering up, so Yogi and I would stop by his office, stick our heads through the door and tell him, "Don't worry, Ralph. We'll start winning."

We had a 9 and 19 record for the Grapefruit League, but all that was washed away when the regular season started. We flew back to New York to open against the Minnesota Twins. The day was cold and windy and held the crowd down to 14,607, but sitting in a box next to the Yankee dugout were three distinguished ladies, the widows of John McGraw, Babe Ruth, and Lou Gehrig. Commissioner Ford Frick and the American League president, Joe Cronin, passed out the rings and watches and raised the 1960 pennant on the flagpole in center field. Roger received his Most

Valuable Player trophy, and then the season was under-
way—badly and slowly.

The game was scoreless for six innings, but Pedro Ramos
finished with a three-hitter and beat Whitey Ford, 6-0. In
the first fourteen days, we had nine games postponed
because of the rain and cold. After going hitless the first two
games, I hit four homers in four days, and in Baltimore a
story noted that I was now "eight games ahead of the pace
set by Babe Ruth when he hit 60 in 1927." That was worth a
few laughs. The date was April 21. We had played a total of
six games.

What most people forget is how slowly Roger started
the season. He was hitting .161 after ten games. I had seven
homers before Maris hit his first, against Detroit on April
26, and the front office made an appointment for him to
be examined by an eye doctor. The timing was brutal. That
week Roger broke out of his slump, batting over .400 with
four homers. Then the night after his exam he couldn't
play because the eyedrops had blurred his vision. Houk was
furious. "We finally get Roger hitting," he said, "and he
shows up blind."

I can't really point to a date and say this is when the
Home Run Derby began. Roger and I both got hot at bat
and the ball started jumping into the seats. The Yankees
would run away from Detroit in the pennant race, and in
any other year they would have been writing ballads about
the Tigers. Norm Cash won the batting title and hit 41
home runs. Rocky Colavito hit 45 and Al Kaline had 19 for
a three-man total of 105.

That gives you an idea of how big a year we were having. Maris and Mantle combined for a total of 115 homers,
breaking the record Ruth and Gehrig had owned since
1927.

From the end of May through June, Roger was in what
today's athletes call a "zone." We just called it a groove. He
connected for 24 homers in 38 games, over a period of five

weeks. By June, the stories on the pursuit of Ruth's record were rolling out of the typewriters like peanuts out of a machine. On July 19, Ford Frick announced that no batter would be credited with breaking Ruth's record unless he did so within 154 games—the number played in the pre-expansion schedule. He added that if the record was passed after the 154-game point, the number would be accompanied by a "distinguishing mark." This turned out to be an asterisk.

At that point, we were both ahead of the Babe's pace, Maris with thirty-five home runs and thirty-three for me. Between Memorial Day and Labor Day, we both homered in the same game thirteen times.

Any day that one of us didn't drive one out was worth a headline: M&M BOYS FAIL TO CONNECT. To gain a sense of what this long-ball circus generated, you have to remember that when Ruth set his record and when DiMaggio compiled his streak, there was no television news, and only a small corner of the map where major league games were seen. The planet had changed since the heyday of Ruth. With each passing week, there were more cameras and tape recorders in the Yankee clubhouse, more people bearing pads and pencils.

In Dallas, a stripper adopted the name of Mickey Maris. Newspapers started holding contests, with cash prizes for the reader who could predict how many homers the two of us would hit.

In 1927, Ruth's relentless march to the record was of interest mainly to himself. He already held it, with fifty-nine.

I was having the time of my life. It was an adventure, a remarkable thing to be a part of, and so there won't be any doubt, I wanted to be the one to break Ruth's record. But I recognized that the heavier pressure was on Roger. He was in front after mid-July, he was less known, a guy who just sort of popped up out of nowhere. At least, that was how the press portrayed him. I mean, he had won the MVP award the previous year. He wasn't exactly a mysterious stranger.

Not many people are prepared for a fame this intense, and it came almost overnight to Roger, who never wanted to be a special person. No player ever accomplished so much and enjoyed it so little. As he closed in on the record, the buildup engulfed him. He tried to blend in with the scenery, but it wasn't easy.

I think Maris was resented because he had the irreverence to attack the record of baseball's greatest hero, but he had none of the gaudy color that the fans had come to expect of their idols. He was uncomfortable in the spotlight, where Ruth had reveled in it; too nervous to enjoy the cheers when he heard them, and unable to ignore the boos that came when the cheering stopped. As the home runs mounted, he went after the record with a sullen intensity and his hair started falling out.

The newsmen and television reporters were at him constantly. He had to answer more questions than a suspect in a bank robbery. And at times he was treated with about as much courtesy. Once, a Japanese sports editor sent a list of eighteen questions to the Associated Press in New York, asking that they be put to the two of us. I treated the request as a joke and breezed through it. After hearing five or six, Maris blurted out, "This is driving me nuts."

The AP reporter replied, "That's the next question. They want to know how you're reacting to all this."

A writer traveling with the Yankees asked Roger if he played around on the road. "I'm married," he snapped.

"I'm married," said the writer, "but I still play around."

"That's your business," said Maris, walking away.

But I had been through this drill once, having hit fifty-two homers in 1956 and kept even or ahead of the pace until September. That month always had been the wall for home run hitters in the past—namely Jimmie Foxx and Hank Greenberg, who both had a shot at the record and finished with fifty-eight.

In '27, Ruth had delivered seventeen home runs, a monster of a finishing kick. He actually hit his last twenty-four in a period of forty-one games, a time when the long season has taken its toll, you feel nicked and bruised, the legs have lost their spring, the mind is tired. Yet Roger kept responding to the challenge.

For most of the summer and into the stretch it was the two of us racing the legend of Ruth for the home run title of all time. Then I gradually began to fade, troubled earlier by the shoulder problem and then by a pulled muscle in my forearm. Houk offered to rest me for a day or two. I said, no, I'll bunt, I'll field, I'll get on base. I wasn't quite ready to concede the record, but I can count, and the odds were much better for Maris. When the Yankees arrived in Minneapolis for a series in August, Maris had fifty-one homers to my forty-seven.

On the day I hit my forty-eighth, off Jim Kaat of the Twins at Metropolitan Stadium, I told Roger, "Well, I got my man. The pressure's off me. Now it's up to you." I was kidding on the square. When Ruth hit his sixtieth, Lou Gehrig had produced forty-seven.

For Roger, the pressure never ceased. In Chicago, a writer asked him if he *really* wanted to break the record, inasmuch as Ruth was a great man and all. "Maybe I'm not a great man," said Maris, honestly enough, "but I damned well want to break the record."

And so he did. His detractors pointed out that Maris had four more games than the Babe, but they ignored the fact that Ruth never saw the depth of pitching that Maris did. The Babe never faced such bull pens, nor did he play at night, when the percentages are against the hitter.

I thought Roger's achievement was the greatest of my time. It may seem strange today, but he hardly made a dime out of the record. You heard so much that year about Maris and Mantle, that the sales of M&M candies were way up. But no one ever asked us about an endorsement. Today a smart agent would jump all over that one. It didn't matter to Roger, who was like the mouse who didn't want the cheese, he just wanted to get his tail out of the trap. "When the trouble came," he told me later, "I just wanted to get out of the pubic eye." You can get a real insight into an athlete's state of mind when he no longer cares about money. To Roger, "trouble" meant the reporters who were coming at him in waves, the strangers who wouldn't leave him alone, and even the great players of another generation who wanted to protect the Babe's record.

Rogers Hornsby, a colorful old goat who was in the Hall of Fame, told reporters how Maris could be stopped: "Throw the first two inside and make him foul them. Then come outside so he can't pull (the ball). It would be a shame if Ruths' record got broken by a .270 hitter."

"[Bleep] Hornsby," said Maris. "They been trying that on me all year and you see how it works."

When the 154th game of the regular season rolled around—his last chance to beat the record without an asterisk—the Yankees were playing in Baltimore, Ruth's birthplace. Maris had 58 homers and needed 2 more to tie Ruth under the new rules. He lined out his first time up. He homered for number 59. He lined out again. He dribbled a Hoyt Wilhelm knuckler back to the mound in his last turn at bat, and the Baltimore crowd stood on its feet and cheered his effort. This was Babe Ruth country and Maris had won them over. With 5 games left in the regular season, he stroked number 60 off Jack Fisher, of the Orioles, in Yankee Stadium. Mrs. Ruth was there to congratulate him. Then he did something only Roger could have done. Needing one more to break it, with four games left, he asked Ralph for a day off. His wife was in town and he wanted to spend the time with her. He returned to the ballpark on Friday, went hitless, then homerless on Saturday. He still needed one on the final day. He flied out his first time up, but in the fourth inning he got under a 2-0 pitch from Boston's Tracy Stallard and sent it sailing into the lower deck in right field.

That was number 61 and in my mind the record was his. Forget the asterisk and the die-hard oldtimers and the Roaring Twenties. Roger had given a new baseball generation something for their own memories, for the glory of their own times.

I finished with fifty-four, and I was thrilled—a word I don't use much—to be a part of it, part of the grandest two-man show over one extraordinary season that baseball had ever seen. With me batting behind him, Roger didn't get an intentional walk all season.

I'm sure some of the writers and broadcasters would have enjoyed a good feud, but there wasn't any. End of story. Roger and I were roommates that entire season, along with Bob Cerv, and we never exchanged a cross word. I wish I had broken the record, but I didn't, and neither did anyone else. I'm glad for Roger. He earned it, and I don't want to hear any baloney about expansion having watered down the pitching, or the travel being easier, or the ball and bats being livelier. He did this incredible deed with most of the country rooting against him, and he did it without being Babe Ruth.

One thing the home run duel didn't cause was a problem on the team or in the clubhouse. The players wanted both of us to break the record, but the sentiment leaned my way. For one thing, I was a switch-hitter and that figured to help me. But the main factor was the most obvious: I had been a Yankee forever, and Roger was in his second year, one of the two players in the lineup not a product of our farm system. The other was Clete Boyer.

You can't imagine the kind of season we had getting overshadowed, but that is what happened. How many people remember that in 1961 the Yankees won 109 games and hit 240 homers as a team? We had so much power that a guy like Moose Skowron had to bat seventh. And poor Whitey. All of his career he had wanted to win 20 games. That year he won 25 and lost only four and went almost unnoticed.

I'll say this for the Babe. He probably got more publicity that year than he did when he set the record. He got a ton of ink for a guy who had been dead since 1948.

But let me tell you about living with Roger. A friend of ours, a union guy and a devout Yankee fan named Julie Isaacson, found an apartment for Maris and Cerv in Queens. Roger wanted his family to stay in Kansas City, where they owned a nice house and the kids had room to play and the streets were safe. My wife stayed in Dallas with our kids for some of the same reasons. Plus, Merlyn hated to fly and that was a hard train ride from Dallas to New York, three days with four boys. We had lived in New Jersey one year, and she didn't feel very secure when the team was on the road. One night she was feeding the baby, Billy, and heard a noise downstairs. She figured there was a burglar in the house. She cradled the baby with one hand and had a .45 in the other, and as she tiptoed down the stairs the gun accidentally went off, blowing a hole in the wall. There was no burglary, but Merlyn pretty much decided that from then on, the family would stay in Texas.

It was Roger's idea to invite me to move in with him and Cerv. In fact, he almost insisted on it. I may have had the image, but Maris really was the all-American boy. He worried about how much it was costing me to live at the Hotel St. Moritz. He worried about the hours I kept and the night spots that were so convenient.

Roger told me it was nice and quiet in Queens, and normally I wouldn't have listed that as an attraction. But he caught me in the right mood. I was making $65,000 that year, and it wasn't unusual for me to have dinner and drinks with friends and some of the players and pick up a tab for a thousand bucks.

When John Blanchard was a rookie, and nervous about getting around, I talked him into staying with me. When he checked into the hotel, the desk clerk told him the room rate was $125 a night. The next thing I knew he had picked up his bags and was heading for the door. "I'm gonna ease on down the street, Mick," he said. "This place is too rich for my blood."

I said, "Tell you what. I'll pay the hundred and you pay the twenty-five." That's how we did it. But, hell, we could eat a week at the apartment in Queens for what a hamburger from room service cost.

One of Roger's selling points was the press wouldn't find us out there, and they didn't. There were good restaurants around the corner and we kept the fridge stocked with sandwiches and pizza. Cerv was a light-hearted guy who would fit in anywhere. He just about grew himself out of the big leagues. When he was with the expansion team in Houston a year later, they couldn't find pants big enough to fit his thighs. So they tore up two pair of pants and sewed them together.

Off the field, we were leading what passed for a fairly normal life. One day we went shopping at a supermarket near the apartment, Roger and me both pushing carts, loading up with ham and beer and other essentials. There were two stockboys arranging the shelves, one passing cans to the other on a ladder. We came around the corner and the kid on the ground said, "Hey, there's Maris and Mantle."

The other one said, "Man, you're crazy. What the hell would Roger Maris and Mickey Mantle be doing in Queens?" Then we turned down their aisle, he saw us and fell off the ladder, with cans and boxes scattering in all directions.

I hit my fifty-fourth homer on September 23 in Boston, and did nothing the rest of the week. My legs were hurting and I was fighting a bad case of the flu. On the train home from Boston, I sat with Mel Allen, our announcer, and he gave me the name of a doctor whose office was off Central Park West.

It turns out that he was one of those celebrity feel-good doctors, who had a miracle shot for whatever ailed you. He used a syringe that looked as large as a bicycle pump, and then he injected me too high on my right hip with a needle that wasn't sterilized. The pain was so bad, I swear I think he actually hit the bone.

I said to him, "Hot damn, that hurts," and he assured me I would be all right momentarily. He told me to walk it off, don't catch a cab. I almost passed out on the street.

I had checked back into the St. Moritz because Merlyn was coming up for the World Series. I had to have the desk send someone out to meet her train. The next morning I found myself at Lenox Hill Hospital, where my knee had been operated on ten years earlier. The doctors cut a three-inch star over the hip bone, then lanced the infection and let it drain. I watched Roger get his sixtieth and sixty-first homers from my hospital bed. I saw a bunch of the guys push him back onto the field so he could tip his cap to the crowd at Yankee Stadium.

As eventful as the season had been, I was determined to play against the Cincinnati Reds in the World Series. I was sick and weak from the abscess and, I swear, the hole in my hip was big enough for a golf ball. I was in no shape to do much of anything, but I told Ralph I planned on being in the lineup. We still had to atone for last year's loss to the Pirates.

As it turned out, my body couldn't afford the price my mind was willing to pay. I missed the first two games as the teams split. Whitey pitched a shutout in the opener, 2-0, with Skowron and Howard hitting homers with the bases empty.

The Reds bounced back the next day with a 6-2 win behind Joey Jay, who had the distinction of being the first Little League graduate to reach the major leagues. Pitching was clearly the strength of the National League champions. The Reds had quality players in Frank Robinson, Vada Pinson and Gordy Coleman, but most of all they had Fred Hutchinson, a manager both feared and respected, who had been a hot-tempered pitcher with the Tigers.

There was a travel day before the third game, at Crosley Field, and with the extra rest I made up mind to play, still limping and hurting. The wound was still draining, and Dr.

Gaynor dressed it with thick layers of gauze over the incision. I went hitless in four times at bat and only had one fly ball hit to me the entire game. I was lucky. Maris won the game with a homer in the ninth.

I was getting treated in the clubhouse before Game 4 when Houk got a good look at the hole in my hip. He said, "Goddamn, man, you can't play with something like that."

I said, "I'm playing."

Ralph said, "Mickey, I'm not gonna let you play. I'll get you in as a pinch hitter, I promise."

I said, "I'm playing."

He walked a few feet away and talked quietly to Doc Gaynor, who told him there was no reason I couldn't play, if I could tolerate the pain. There was no risk of any permanent injury, or that sort of thing.

Game 4 was runless when Roger led off the fourth inning with a walk. Then I drilled a line drive off the wall in left-center, normally a cinch double. This time I had to stop at first. I stood there gritting my teeth, breaking into a cold sweat, blood rolling down my leg and soaking through my uniform. Houk pulled me for a pinch runner and later in the inning Roger scored the first run.

I went back into the clubhouse and had yards of bloody gauze unwrapped and the bandage changed, then I watched us pull away for a 7-0 win. I was back on the training table after the game, and several of the players walked over to take a look. Tony Kubek said you could see the bone in my hip.

But the real story that day was Whitey Ford, who pitched five shutout innings before a foot injury forced him to leave. That ran his string to thirty-two scoreless innings and broke the record Babe Ruth had set in his days as a Boston Red Sox pitcher. In the same year, Ruth had lost his records for most home runs and for shutout innings in the World Series; 1961 was not a good year for the Babe.

We were now ahead three games to one and looking for a quick kill. I was back on the bench for Game 5, along with Yogi, who was nursing a stiff shoulder. Ralph felt some pressure to get it over with because the squad was thinning out. Bob Cerv was out with a bad knee, Ford was finished, and Bill Stafford had a sore wrist.

The Reds were hoping to get another clutch game from Joey Jay, but our "second string" went wild in a 13-5 victory. Hector Lopez, playing right field for Berra, drove in five runs with a triple and a homer, and John Blanchard, batting fourth in my spot, contributed three hits, including a double and a homer. The only sour note was Ralph Terry getting knocked out, giving up six hits in less than three innings. Bud Daley came on to go the rest of the way and get the win in relief.

Fred Hutchinson didn't go down softly. He used eight pitchers, and four of them didn't get through an inning.

That was the way the World Series ended, with me playing in just two games and Maris hitting a puny .105. But was it an anticlimax? No, it was really a proper ending. Two guys had hogged the headlines all year, now some of the others had a chance to shine. Ralph Houk had proven himself in his rookie season as the manager of the Yankees. He called 1961 his greatest year in baseball.

I don't like to single out teams because I played on so many that you could call "great" without being accused of overkill. But the 1961 Yankees are my favorite. Seven players on that team hit twenty or more home runs. And I know people will always think of home runs when they think of Roger Maris, but he was a complete player, who never made a mistake.

He's another fellow who ought to be in the Hall of Fame and I think it's a scandal that the writers have kept him out. In a curious way, Maris made me more popular in New York than I had ever been. They wouldn't forgive Roger for not being Babe Ruth. They finally forgave me for not being Joe DiMaggio. For the first time they saw me as an underdog, making it a race, playing hurt. In a way I had not heard before, they cheered me for what I did and what I might have done.

# REMATCH BY THE BAY

## 1962—YANKEES 4, GIANTS 3

Eleven years after we had last played them, and four years after they gave up Manhattan, the Bronx, and Staten Island, too, we met the Giants again in the World Series. In 1951, they had caught the Dodgers at the wire and beat them in a playoff. In 1962, the Giants had caught the Dodgers at the wire and beat them in a playoff.

Was it Yogi who said, "It seems like déjà vu all over again?" No, he didn't, but it was.

Of course, there was this obvious difference. Instead of a Subway Series, this one was transcontinental. These were the San Francisco Giants, and that year they had moved into their handsome new ballpark by the Bay. They didn't know yet what a lemon Candlestick Park would turn out to be.

There were only two members of the 1951 New York Giants still with the team, Willie Mays, rolling along in center field, and Alvin Dark, the former shortstop and now the manager. Only Yogi Berra and I were still around from the '51 Yankees—Whitey Ford was in the army during the '51 and '52 seasons.

So I looked on this World Series trip as a sentimental journey and a circular one. Willie had come to San Francisco, one of the most inviting cities on the planet, and the fans had dared him to prove he was worthy of being compared to a hometown idol named Joe DiMaggio. There it was. At a stage of his career when he should have been soaking up the glory, he found himself in the same shadow I had been under as a rookie. Some of the fans heckled Mays and they adopted as their favorites Willie McCovey and Orlando Cepeda, both great players who had no New York connection.

One line sort of summed it up. A few years earlier, San Francisco had been host to the premier of the Soviet Union, and banners were flown and the sidewalks spruced up and they gave him a polite welcome. "This is a strange city," said a visiting newspaper editor. "They cheer Khrushchev and boo Willie Mays."

Mays and I were friends from our New York days in spite of all the talk of a heated rivalry. Our rivalry was on the golf course, where we hustled each other whenever we got the chance. I wanted to beat Willie, but I would never embarrass him and I didn't like it if someone else did.

I may have done that once, but it wasn't deliberate. The All-Star Game was in San Francisco that summer, and Whitey and I flew out after a Friday game so we could relax and get in a round of golf. Horace Stoneham, the owner of the Giants, arranged for us to play at his club, which was nice of him. The only problem was that we didn't have the right clothes, so we went to the pro shop and bought a couple sweaters, shoes, caps, rented some clubs, had a few drinks, and charged it all to Stoneham's account, which wasn't very nice of us. But they wouldn't take cash and we planned on repaying him. The bill came to about $400.

Later that night, Horace invited us to a cocktail party. I gave Whitey my half of the money and he walked over to him, explained what we had done and handed him the cash. Horace wouldn't take it. Instead, he offered Whitey a wager, double or nothing. If he faced Mays in the All-Star Game and got him out, we kept the money. If Mays got a hit, we owed him $800.

Now even though we seldom saw the Giants, when we did Mays always hit Ford as if the ball were on a tee. His average against him in the All-Star Game must have been about .900.

But Whitey couldn't resist a challenge and he was gleeful when he came back and told me he had accepted on my behalf. I told him, no, hell, no, I didn't want any part of it, but Whitey was confident. "Look at it this way," he said. "I might not even pitch tomorrow."

The headline on the next day's sports page rid us of any such hope: SPAHN, FORD TO START ALL-STAR GAME.

I could afford to lose my half, I mean, $400 wasn't going to hurt me. But I hated to lose a sucker bet and this was one of them. And I knew Whitey would be rattled because he really had no idea how to pitch to Willie.

Sure enough, Mays came up in the first inning with two out and Roberto Clemente on second base with a double. Ford wasn't worried about the run, he was thinking about the bet. A walk wouldn't count so he had to work on him. Willie fouled off two pitches and Whitey looked around and saw me with my hands on my knees, glaring at him. He decided to take a chance. He swore he had never thrown a spitter in a game, but he had played around with it. The problem was that he didn't know where the ball would go. Sometimes they broke and sometimes they didn't. And nothing was easier to hit than a spitter that came in flat and straight.

He figured if he was ever going to try one in a game, now was the time. So he spit into his left hand, pretended to wipe it off on his shirt, and cut loose. The pitch was going right at Willie's hand and as it neared the plate he jumped out of the way. Then, at the last instant, the ball just dropped three feet and sailed over the center of the plate and the umpire jerked his right hand and yelled, "Strike three!"

I came off the field laughing and clapping, and as Mays and Ford passed each other Willie asked, frowning, "What the hell is he so happy about?" Whitey said, "I'll explain it later."

But it didn't dawn on me right away how it must have looked to Willie and the crowd. It looked as if I was all tickled about Mays striking out because of the big rivalry, and in the dugout when Whitey mentioned my reaction I slapped my forehead and sputtered, "Aw, no . . . I didn't . . . how could I . . . what a dumb thing." Anyway, we kept our money and later Whitey told Mays why I was acting like an idiot and he just laughed.

I felt for Willie because 1962 had been a rough year for him off the field. His ex-wife had won a $15,000-a-year settlement—big money then—plus legal fees, and her lawyer was suing him for payment. The papers said that he was more than $100,000 in debt and his attorneys had urged him to file for bankruptcy (but in the end he didn't need to). He led the league in homers, batted .304, and fainted from nervous exhaustion in the dugout in September.

We had won the pennant by five games and I collected my third MVP trophy, but I didn't turn any cartwheels over it. For one thing, I couldn't. I was trying to beat out an infield hit in May, put on a finishing burst, and felt the hamstring pull in my right leg—the bad one. I tried to ease off by taking a couple of awkward hops and tore two ligaments and some cartilage in my good leg. I missed a month and when I came back I couldn't do much right away except pinch-hit.

The odds were not very high that we could top our storybook season of 1961, with Maris breaking Ruth's record and all. On opening day of '62, Roger and I both homered, along with Moose Skowron, but that was definitely not an omen of things to come. Roger's home run totals dropped from 61 to 33. Mine were off from 54 to 30. Whitey's victory total shrank from 25 to 17. And the Yankees went from 109 wins to 96.

In the National League, it was uncanny how similar the season was to 1951. The Dodgers had a comfortable lead most of the season, then they lost Sandy Koufax to an injury in July. They lost ten of their last thirteen games, and the final four in a row to blow a four-game lead. Mays hit a home run in the ninth inning of the Giants' last game to force a playoff.

Alvin Dark did a very smart thing with Mays. He made him the team captain and there was a little history behind that move. Willie went through a rookie slump just as I did, except his came right after the Giants had called him up from Minneapolis. The veterans on the team rode him hard, and Leo Durocher walked into the clubhouse one day and found him crying. The action of the game came so easily to Mays, but the fringe stuff sometimes confused him.

When Durocher asked him what was wrong, Mays said, "I don't belong here. I'm not ready for the big leagues. Please send me back where I came from."

Leo was no fool and he wasn't going to let Mays go anywhere. He said, "Son, you're a Giant and you're going to stay a Giant." Mays was twenty and he believed he wasn't wanted. He was wrong and Monte Irvin, his friend and teammate, told him so, but he had to hear it from Durocher.

Leo constantly stroked him, and predicted greatness for him, and didn't concern himself with how that went down with the other players. He knew Mays was the team's future.

Later, though, Horace Stoneham decided that Leo was so openly protective of Mays, so partial to him, that the relationship had somehow hurt the club. When Bill Rigney became manager, the owner gave him some advice: "Treat

Willie like any other member of the team. We want everybody to be happy."

When Rigney was fired by the Giants, he was asked what he thought was his biggest mistake as a manager. "I worried about too many ball players' feelings," he said, bluntly. "And I let Willie think I didn't care about him." I read those words and they stayed with me. There is a lesson in them for the people in sports—and anywhere else. We all want to know that we are needed. An insecure person, as many athletes are, want to hear it every day.

When the Giants picked up stakes in '58 and landed in San Francisco, Mays bumped up against the DiMaggio Factor. Joe's family owned a restaurant on Fisherman's Wharf. He and his brothers, Vince and Dom, had come up from the sandlots to star on the city's minor league team, the Seals, and then to the majors. Confusion set in again with Mays about belonging and feeling needed. Then Alvin Dark, his old teammate, a guy Willie truly liked and respected, showed up to manage the Giants.

Dark was fairly complicated himself. He had been to college, and had made the all-America team as a halfback at LSU. He was quiet and religious, one of the first baseball players I can remember who said he tithed and flat-out talked about his belief in God. That was one side of him.

After the Giants had left twelve men on base in a game against the Phillies, and loused up the game, he picked up a chair in the clubhouse and threw it against the wall. Unluckily, his little finger got caught in the hinge and the tip of it went with the chair.

Then he escalated the Giants' ongoing war with the Dodgers. Maury Wills was hot on the bases at the time. Alvin found a way to cool him off. He watered the infield until the basepaths looked like a rice paddy. This so offended the Dodgers that one of their executives referred to Dark as a "Mississippi mudcat," a major insult since Alvin was from Louisiana.

In Pittsburgh, his big hitters were knocked down by the

Pirates, and Alvin promised he would take the law into his own hands if the dusters didn't stop. The league promptly fined him for saying out loud what managers usually kept in the clubhouse. In Philadelphia, Dark was thrown out of a game after one of his players was thrown at, and he told the umpire that the Phillies' pitcher would get plugged the next time he came to bat. And he was, even if Alvin wasn't there to see it.

So the Giants were again a team with a temper, as they had been under Durocher and Dressen. They could match us in power with Mays, McCovey, Cepeda, Jim Davenport, Felipe Alou, and Ed Bailey. They were at least as deep in starters, with a staff led by Juan Marichal, the guy with a leg kick the Radio City Rockettes would envy. Then they had Jack Sanford and the left-handers, Billy Pierce and Bill O'Dell. Coming out of the bull pen was our old pal and former teammate, Don Larsen.

The Yankees were in transition. We went into the Series with a rookie in left field, Tom Tresh, the son of the long-time White Sox catcher, Mike Tresh. His natural position was shortstop and he would soon move out Tony Kubek. But his dad had urged him to be versatile. "You never know," said Mike, "when you'll get a ballclub that has someone like Luke Appling [who was the White Sox shortstop for fifteen years]. Guys go bad sitting on the bench." Clete Boyer was now our starting third baseman. We had Phil Linz and Joe Pepitone in the wings.

Yogi was a year away from hanging it up. He caught a few games, played some outfield, pinch-hit, but mostly watched and cheered. He would get into two games and go 0 for 2.

Otherwise, there was a kind of nice roundness to this World Series. Mike Tresh was in the box seats at Candlestick Park to see his son play. Mays, the last survivor of the Miracle of Coogan's Bluff in '51, was in center field—so was I—and the Yankees had Edward Charles Ford on the mound.

Talk about honors creeping up on you. Whitey was

now officially the greatest pitcher in World Series history with nine wins, more than Christy Mathewson, Lefty Grove, or Babe Ruth.

We had jumped ahead in the first when Maris doubled in two runs, but the Giants got one of them back when Jose Pagan put down a perfect bunt to squeeze home Mays in the second. The run was the first in thirty-three and a third innnings off Ford, who now owned the record set by Ruth, when the Babe was a left-handed pitcher for the Red Sox and hit home runs only in his spare time.

No National League team had scored against the native New Yorker since the Braves in 1958. Of course, he hadn't been pitching against Mays, who singled three times and drove in the second run to tie the game in the third. By then we had looked it up: Willie was six-for-seven off Whitey in All-Star play.

The Giants were supposed to be mentally weary after their best-of-three playoff with the Dodgers, but they looked like acrobats to us. Alou played the drive by Maris in the first inning off the cyclone fence in right to hold him to a double, instead of a homer. Then he made a diving catch off the grass in short right to rob Tresh of a hit.

Ford and O'Dell kept it tight until the seventh. Then Boyer, the guy Stengel had lifted for a pinch hitter in his first at bat in a World Series, tagged O'Dell for a tie-breaking homer to left. We added two in the eighth and one in the ninth to wrap up a 6-2 win for Whitey, his tenth. The last out was a lazy fly to center off the bat of Harvey Kuenn, the former American League batting champ at Detroit.

As the ball settled into my glove, Whitey never looked around. He just cleared his desk and left the office. Nobody made a fuss. Elston just gave him a slap on the bottom as he strode toward the dugout. The body language said, these are the Yankees. Winning a World Series game wasn't new to us.

At the start of the seventh, two fans in the bleachers

unfurled a banner that said: WELCOME GIANT-KILLERS, NEW YORK YANKEES. The ushers took it away from them.

Whitey told the press that Mays had been hitting his curve in the All-Star Games, so today he started him off with fastballs—"and he hit those, too. I finally got him with a slider." He only threw two curves all day. A left-hander couldn't throw curves in that stadium with the wind swirling from left to right. The wind took away his best pitch and he still won.

Every fly ball was an adventure in San Francisco. When they built the new stadium at a romantic spot called Candlestick Point, no one was aware of any strange wind cycles. They leveled a mountain to make room for the parking lot and, I guess, to improve the view of the Bay, and then they discovered that the mountain had been blocking the wind.

The story was that when one of the front-office people stopped by to check on the construction, he saw pieces of equipment flying around and workers holding onto some of the girders. "Does the wind always blow like that?" he asked.

"Only between one and five in the afternoon," said an engineer. Of course, you had to play mostly day games in San Francisco. At night, the temperatures were chilly in the spring and early fall and sometimes in July.

Both managers, Dark and Ralph Houk, had their big winners ready for Game 2, Jack Sanford, who had won twenty-four for the Giants, against Ralph Terry, who led our staff with twenty-three. These were two right-handed bulldogs.

In the bottom of the first, Chuck Hiller doubled, was bunted to third, and scored on Felipe Alou's grounder. You didn't figure that run was all Sanford would need, but it was. Willie McCovey's home run to lead off the seventh just gave the fans an excuse to warm their hands. That was the final score, 2-0, and the Series was tied.

The game lasted only two hours and eleven minutes.

The time passes fast when you get held to three hits. I doubled to right with two out in the ninth, but Sanford got Roger on an infield grounder. We had one other runner reach second.

Now the fun really started. The Giants returned to New York in their San Francisco uniforms, trimmed in black and gold. Mixed emotions? They ran wild. In many ways, the Giants had been New York's true love. They had been there first, hadn't been inept or goofy as the Dodgers were for so long, and they won without the arrogance people expected of the Yankees.

Ruth, Gehrig, and DiMaggio were larger than life. But the Giants had their own Hall of Fame: Mathewson, John McGraw, Bill Terry, Mel Ott, Carl Hubbell, Ernie Lombardi. Rogers Hornsby, and Johnny Mize started their careers as Giants. And the great names: Iron Man McGinnity, Dummy Taylor, Van Lingle Mungo, and, briefly, Jim Thorpe, the Carlisle Indian.

Once Willie Mays had played stickball with the kids in the neighborhood. New York still loved Willie, but the rest of them were strangers and the Mets had moved into the Polo Grounds.

In Game 3, Billy Pierce and Bill Stafford threw shutout ball for six innings. We scored three times in the seventh on three singles, an error, and a hit batsman. The middle of our order—Tresh, Mantle, Maris—had the hits and scored the runs. Roger made a smart play when he tagged up and beat the throw to third after Mays hauled down Howard's drive to deep center. This was what so many fans missed about Maris, but not his teammates. He could do everything. He scored when the Giants failed to turn a double play. That was the ball game.

Stafford had a one-hitter through seven and a two-hitter through eight and a shutout until two were out in the ninth, when Ed Bailey homered with Mays on base. He pitched the last inning and a third after getting drilled on the left shin by Felipe Alou's line drive back to the mound.

The ball rebounded halfway to the plate, but he pounced on it and got the out at first. He hobbled around in circles for a minute, then sat down as the trainer knelt beside him and made sure nothing was broken. Then he went back and finished his chores.

Pierce pitched well, except for the one inning, giving up five hits. He had been a rookie with Detroit in 1945 when they played the Cubs in the World Series. Traded to the White Sox, he gave them ten years of class, but worked only three innings of relief when they met the Dodgers in '59. He had already won two hundred games, sixteen of them for the Giants that season.

This day he has to go up against a twenty-four-year-old kid who wouldn't be deprived of his first World Series win. As a rookie, Stafford pitched against the Pirates and a year later against the Reds, but had no decisions. Now he did.

In the fourth game, Whitey returned to try and hike our lead to 3 and 1, going against the Giants' colorful young right-hander, Marichal. Neither starter would be around when the game was decided. Ralph sent up Yogi to bat for Ford in the sixth, after Boyer had singled in two runs, looking for a big inning. Larsen came in to face his old battery-mate and walked Yogi to load the bases. Then he got out of it when Kubek bounced to Cepeda, with Larsen covering first.

The score was 2-2 in the top of the seventh, when the wheels started spinning. Houk brought in Jim Coates and he walked one, struck out one, and gave up a double to Matty Alou, batting for Jose Pagan. Dark sent up Ed Bailey, a left-handed hitter, to bat for Larsen, and Houk countered by bringing in a southpaw, Marshall Bridges.

So Dark replaced Bailey with Bob Nieman and Ralph gave the signal to walk him and load the bases. Ernie Bowman ran for Nieman and the next hitter was Chuck Hiller, the second baseman, what we call a banjo hitter. His average for the Series was .154. His home run total for the past season, including the playoff, was three.

On a 1-1 count, Bridges threw him a high fastball, and it was next seen settling into the right-field stands. Only eight players had ever hit home runs with the bases full in a World Series, and six of them were Yankees. Surprisingly, no National Leaguer had ever hit one before Hiller. The final score was 7-3, and the win was credited to Don Larsen on the sixth anniversary of his perfect game, a nice twist for him. It was a brand new Series at two apiece.

Rain postponed Game 5 for a day, then Ralph Terry and Tom Tresh teamed up to beat the Giants, 5-3. Terry, my fellow Okie from the town of Big Cabin, pitched a gritty game, hanging in there despite giving up eight hits, including a homer by Jose Pagan. Ralph carried the scars from four World Series losses, the most recent in San Francisco. This win was his first.

Jack Sanford had a three-hitter going until the eighth, when a three-run homer by Tresh broke a 2-2 tie and put the game away. Tresh was a cinch to win Rookie of the Year honors and was now hitting .400 in the Series.

This was a game we had to have. We didn't want to get back to that wind tunnel needing two wins and having to face Pierce, who hadn't lost at Candlestick in twelve decisions that year. Sanford had put a collar on me, Maris, Howard, and Skowron, and struck out ten batters. But he couldn't stop the son of Mike Tresh. The kid had a double and a walk to go with his homer, accounted for four of the runs, and laid down a bunt that made the other one possible.

The Giants threatened in the ninth and scored a run on McCovey's double and Tom Haller's single, but Terry retired the last two hitters on a grounder and a liner to Maris in right. As he walked wearily off the field, over the public address system came the old familiar song from *Show Boat*:

> *Many a heart is aching,*
> *if we could read them all—*

*Many the heart that is breaking,*
*after the ball . . .*

If that didn't sum up a World Series, I don't know what did. Now it was back to San Francisco, where I hadn't left a darned thing except maybe some rented golf clubs.

The teams traveled on an off day, a Thursday, and then the rains came and fell for three days. When it finally stopped, Whitey took his lumps, ending his five-game winning streak and handing him his first World Series loss in four years, 5-2.

Pierce held us to three hits, one of them a solo homer by Maris, and was still unbeaten in Candlestick Park. In a match between the guy who owns the World Series and the guy who owns the park, something has to give. The Yankees gave and Pierce took it, for his first World Series decision.

With one out in the fourth, Felipe Alou singled and Mays walked. Pitching to Orlando Cepeda, Whitey whirled and tried to pick off Alou at second. The ball got away from him and sailed twenty feet wide of Richardson. The rains of the past three days had left the outfield too soft for lawn mowers. Any ball landing on the high, moist turf stopped dead and by the time Maris could reach it Alou had scored and Mays was standing on third.

In the second inning, Cepeda had singled to end a hitless streak of twenty-nine games against American League pitching in World Series and All-Star competition. Now he lashed a double that scored Mays. When Davenport's single died in the weeds, Cepeda raced home with the third run.

After Maris homered for our first hit in the fifth, an error and a walk put two men on base. But Ralph let Ford bat for himself and Whitey popped up to end the inning.

Then the Giants had their turn. Harvey Kuenn, Chuck Hiller, Felipe Alou, and Cepeda singled and scored two more runs before Ralph went to the mound and made a change. The Series was tied for the third time and there would be a seventh game the next day, a Tuesday. By then, both teams hoped, the field would be dry. Three helicopters had fanned it from above and the ground crew had turned loose several thousand earthworms to bore into the sod, but the field was barely playable.

The last time the Giants had played for a World Championship, there were eight teams in each league and 154 games in a schedule. This time San Francisco had played 162 games in the regular season, 3 in the playoffs and 7 in the World Series. It would take them a record total of 172 games to get to this point and finish second.

It went down to Ralph Terry for us against Jack Sanford and both were brilliant. There was something almost dishonest about the way we slipped across a run in the fifth, on a double-play ball, and no one could have predicted there would be no more scoring.

In that inning, Skowron and Boyer singled and Sanford walked Terry to load the bases with nobody out. Bad things happen when pitchers walk pitchers. So Moose scored as Kubek hit into a double play.

Terry put down the first seventeen Giants to face him before Sanford singled with two out in the sixth. McCovey tripled with two out in the seventh and was stranded. Then in the bottom of the ninth, Felipe Alou's drag bunt gave the Giants their third hit, with one away. Hiller fanned for the second out.

The batter was Willie Mays. On a 2-and-0 count, Willie doubled to right, and Maris fielded it quickly and fired to the relay man, Richardson. When Bobby turned toward home, he saw that Alou had been held at third, and no throw was required.

And that brought the towering Willie McCovey tromping to the plate. A long, long time ago when the Series was not quite two days old, McCovey had smashed a pitch by Terry out of the park as Sanford blanked us, 2-0. McCovey swung and a half-scream came from the crowd as the ball headed for the fence, then curved foul, pushed by the wind.

Looking on from center field, I wondered why Houk didn't walk this monster with first base open. I was still wondering when McCovey hit the second pitch, a rifle shot right into Richardson's glove. It was weird. For just a fraction of an instant, there was no sound and no movement, so quickly had the ball flashed through the air.

Then Terry brandished his fist, tore off his cap and flung it in the air, and the rest of the Yankee players met and collided between the mound and first base.

The World Series had gone seven games and thirteen days and how could you ask for a better ending than a 1-0 high-wire act. Terry had started three times and won twice, and he earned the *Sport* magazine Corvette as the most valuable player. The Yankees had won it all for the twentieth time.

I had another forgettable Series, hitting .120, and the unhappy Maris, playing himself out of New York, hit .174. Willie Mays struggled, too, batting .250 with no homers and one run batted in.

During the final game, I heard a fan yelling at me from the bleachers. He said, "I came out here to see which one of you guys was the better center fielder. But it looks like I have to decide which one is worse." There was a momentary pause and then his foghorn voice echoed:

"Hey, Mantle, you win."

# L.A. LAW

## 1963—DODGERS 4, YANKEES 0

We completed the nostalgia cycle in 1963, when the Yankees met the Los Angeles Dodgers in the World Series. But it wasn't like old times, when they were a bridge away in Brooklyn and we played them four straight years in the early fifties.

From a distance, I had now seen the total remaking of the Dodgers. The old Brooklyn model ran to slashing hitters and runners in the style of Robinson and Snider and Furillo. The new Dodgers were content to steal a run with Maury Wills and Junior Gilliam and Willie Davis, then let Sandy Koufax and Don Drysdale shut down the opposition.

In Los Angeles, the fans called it a "Dodger double" when Wills singled and swiped second. Then he would score on a ground ball, a long fly, a wild pitch, whatever. Somehow Wills would get around the bases and if Koufax was pitching he'd duck into the dugout and say, "There's your run, Sandy."

The Dodgers played smart baseball. A year earlier, Wills

had broken the record of Ty Cobb with 104 stolen bases. It was fair to say that he couldn't have done it without the clever batwork of the number-two hitter, Jim Gilliam, known as Junior.

Patiently, Gilliam took pitches and gave the runner his opportunity to move. He had a good field of vision, enabling him to look for the pitch and see Maury out of the corner of his eye. After a while, Gilliam could almost sense when Wills was going and would hold his swing.

Frank Howard and Tommy Davis could hurt you with their power, and they had raided our roster over the winter and picked up Moose Skowron in a trade for pitcher Stan Williams. I lost another close buddy. The six-seven Howard was a menacing sight, a former Ohio State basketball player. He had led the Dodgers in homers the last two years, with thirty-one and twenty-eight.

But the Dodgers didn't live or die with the long ball. They beat you with the running game and pitching—when they beat you. The Dodgers were catching hell in Los Angeles, as they had in Brooklyn, for not winning the Big Ones. There were the blown leads and the losses in two playoffs in 1951 and 1962, both to the Giants. There were those losses to the Yankees in the World Series, the biggest ones of all.

Walt Alston was in his tenth season and before the opener he was asked if managing was tougher today than when he started. He said, "It hasn't changed. The only thing that changes is your team. In the mid-fifties, we had what is known as a set-eight. With fellows like Snider, Reese, Campanella, Hodges, and so forth, we knew everyday who our starters were going to be. We either won with them or got beat.

"Well, when you're not sure about your set-eight, problems develop. You've got two men for one position, or a player who must be removed for defensive purposes in the late innings, or another who can't hit left-handers. These things pose trouble for a manager, but they were trouble ten years ago, too."

Ralph Houk and Alston had the same philosophy, unlike Stengel, who loved to move the pawns around and probably platooned as much as any manager who ever lived.

I was eager to meet up again with Koufax, who had been a bonus baby too wild to let pitch in 1955, and Drysdale, who had gotten into one game in '56. Now they were just about the most feared one-two punch on the mound in baseball.

Sandy had been awesome that year with a 25-and-5 record, and Drysdale had won 19. Don was among the fiercest competitors I ever saw. In the spring, on a whim, I had dragged a bunt against him for a single. I did it because I knew I could. When he reached the bag, a couple of steps behind me, he planted his foot on top of mine and gave his spikes a twist. Our faces were inches away, and I looked at him with honest surprise. "Don't ever do that to me again," he bellowed.

I said, "I won't," and I meant it.

As he walked away, Don turned and said, "And I won't forget that you did it this time." Before the third game of the Series, he walked over and poked me in the ribs and asked, "Where do you want it?" He must have softened up because he didn't plug me.

Our pitching wasn't exactly shabby, either. In fact, it had to carry us because injuries really dogged us. We went through the last four months of the season without starting our eight regulars in the same game.

The first week in June, I tried to climb the chain-link fence in Baltimore to haul in a drive by Brooks Robinson, and I caught my spikes in the wire. I wound up with a broken bone in my left foot and damaged the cartilage and ligaments in my left knee—my good knee. They carried me off the field and I missed sixty-one games. A lot of people, including me, wondered if my career was over.

But something was going on that season, maybe sympathy for the injuries, or just a reaction to my having been around for thirteen seasons. I was getting applauded and cheered in rival ballparks. In Yankee Stadium, I was getting ovations. I made my return as a pinch hitter in early August, at home, against the Orioles. We had lost the first game of a doubleheader and trailed in the second, 10-9, in the bottom of the seventh.

Ralph told me to hit for the pitcher, and as soon as the fans on the third-base side saw me go to the bat rack they began clapping. The rest of the crowd picked it up. When I took my first step out of the dugout, more than 38,000 fans rose as if on a signal and gave me the loudest reception I had ever heard.

Ralph had warned me not to run hard if I hit a grounder. I was more worried about striking out and looking bad. The pitcher was a left-hander named George Brunet, who would still be pitching twenty years later in the Mexican League, when he was pushing fifty.

I swung at the second pitch and hit a line drive that stayed up just enough to clear the fence in left field. I had hit a lot of home runs a whole lot harder, but this was one of the most dramatic. The fans were up and screaming as I limped around the bases. It tied the score and we went on to win, 11-10. In the clubhouse, the writers asked me about the ovation. I said, "It actually gave me chills. I was shaking. I could feel the bumps rising on my arms. I told myself, 'I'd settle for a single.'" Of the homer, I said, "I didn't think it would go. I didn't think I had pulled it enough. I didn't think it would get into the seats, but I saw the umpire wave his arm and I told myself, 'I'm a lucky stiff. Gee, but I'm a lucky stiff.'"

For the next month I was used only as a pinch hitter and then not very often. I went to bat only seven times in August and was hitless with three walks.

I spent too much time sitting in the dugout, being bored. The troubling thing was, I found myself getting used to it.

So one night, before a game at Baltimore, I went with Whitey and Dale Long to the farm of some friends of ours and we stayed up most of the night drinking wine.

Yankee fans loved to hear the stories about Babe Ruth coming to the park nursing a bad hangover and hitting a home run, or two or three. I had hit a few in that condition myself, and I can tell you, it's overrated. I was in no shape to play the next morning, but I didn't expect to play, anyway.

Not only was I hung over, but I fell half asleep on the bench. We trailed the Orioles 4-1 in the eighth, when Houk woke me to tell me to go hit for the pitcher. I straightened up, smoothed out my cap—Ford had been sitting on it— and started to the plate to face a left-hander, Mike McCormick, with Clete Boyer on base. I heard Whitey yell at me to swing at the first fastball I saw.

The Orioles were aware of the situation. Hank Bauer, who had taken care of me as a rookie, was on their coaching staff. He saw how I looked when I got to the ballpark, and he passed the word. The Orioles didn't expect me to get in the game.

McCormick's first pitch was a high fastball and I remembered Whitey's advice. I jumped on it and lifted a long homer over the left-field fence, right where I had broken my foot in June. That cut the lead to 4-3, and in the press box they spotted Ford in our dugout giving me one of those salaams. In the *Baltimore Sun*, Bob Maisel wrote that the Yankees acted "as if they were celebrating New Year's Eve . . . [Ford] raised his hands over his head, then lowered them to the ground, as though he might be worshipping some god."

When I stumbled into the dugout, I was breathing hard and motioned toward the stands and said to my grinning teammates, "Those people don't know how tough that really was." We went on to win, 5-4, on a homer by Tom Tresh, his second, one from each side of the plate. He was only the third American Leaguer to switch-hit homers in the same game.

The next day I played in the outfield, in center, for the first time since the accident. Ralph was getting me ready for the World Series. I finished the season hitting .314, with 15 home runs, the fewest since my rookie year. I missed 61 games and had only 172 at bats. Between us, Maris and I went to bat 484 times, barely a full season for one player.

Yet the Yankees finished ten and a half games ahead of the second-place White Sox. Elston Howard was voted the league's Most Valuable Player with a .313 average, twenty-eight homers, and eighty-five runs batted in. The depth of our bench and our four starting pitchers were responsible for this pennant. Whitey had a 24-7 record. Young Jim Bouton was 21-7. Ralph Terry won seventeen games and Al Downing, a rookie left-hander who didn't join the team until June, had thirteen.

We were expecting a blue-chip Series. More often than not, it seemed to me, the first game was a duel between southpaws. This one had the players and the fans dry-washing their hands: Ford and Koufax.

The Series opened at Yankee Stadium, and Whitey retired the side in the first inning on two strikeouts and a grounder. He had sent Sandy a message: top that. And darned if he didn't. Koufax struck out the side, Kubek, Richardson swinging, Tresh looking.

That set the tone. Sandy went on to strike out fifteen Yankees to break the record of fourteen that Carl Erskine set against us in 1953, in what seemed like another lifetime. That game was played ten years ago to the day.

With Koufax at the peak of his form, the Dodgers put the game away with four runs in the second inning. Frank Howard drilled a double to left-center in the 460-foot range. The next hitter was Skowron, who had been my teammate for nine years. The Dodgers obtained him to take some pressure off big Frank, but his season had been a nightmare.

He hit .203 and drove in just nineteen runs and the crowds booed him every time his name was announced. In New York, when they yelled his name, stretching it out,

M-o-o-o-s-e, it sounded as if they were booing him. Now he was hearing real boos, and that was exactly what it sounded like.

I felt sorry for Moose, but not for long. I was too busy fielding his single up the middle, which scored the game's first run. Then Dick Tracewski, a good glove man who was starting at second base, singled and John Roseboro, the catcher, unloaded a three-run homer into a fan's lap in the right-field seats.

The Dodgers added a run on three singles in the third, the last one by Skowron bringing in the run. They led, 5-0, and that would be the final score.

Koufax worked fast. He would lean in, get the sign, bring the hands over his head, kick high, and fire. He struck out every regular except Clete Boyer at least once. He fanned Bobby Richardson three times; Kubek, Tresh, and me twice. Each of our pinch hitters went down swinging, and the last one, Harry Bright, broke the record.

There wasn't anything funny about it, except for what Harry said after the game: "I waited all my life to get into a World Series, and when I did everybody was rooting for me to strike out." By then, the Dodgers had the game won and even the Yankee fans wanted to see a record.

You want to know just how dominating Sandy was? Not until the eighth inning did a Dodger outfielder make a putout. That was the inning he also lost his shutout on a two-run homer by Tom Tresh. Our other five hits were singles.

All anyone could talk about after the game was Koufax. "I can see how he won twenty-five games," said Yogi Berra. "What I don't understand is how he lost five."

Sandy was a solemn guy on the mound, but he wasn't humorless. Hank Aaron told me how he once fouled off a dozen pitches looking for one to hit, and Koufax stepped off the mound, rubbed up the ball, and called down to him: "Hank, it's me and you now. I'm going to throw my best fastball right down the middle, and you're either going to hit it out of the park or not out of the park. But there will be no more foul balls." On the next pitch, Aaron popped up.

Two more southpaws started the second game. Houk picked the rookie, Al Downing, to go against the veteran Johnny Podres, a fourteen-game winner in Los Angeles, and the guy not forgotten in Brooklyn. He beat us in the seventh game in 1955, to give Flatbush its only World Championship.

We were in for more of the same. With two on in the first, Maris raced in for a ball hit by Willie Davis, slammed on the brakes, tried to go back, and fell on the seat of his britches. The ball dropped in for a two-run double, giving Podres all the working room he needed. Later, Skowron's homer added a run and Tommy Davis drove in another with his second triple. He took his shutout into the ninth, when Hector Lopez doubled with one out. Alston brought in Ron Perranoski, who gave up a run-scoring single to Elston Howard before closing us out, 4-1.

The cheers for Podres swelled as he went along. The fans booed Alston for taking him out.

In two games, my old pal Skowron had three hits and a homer and a .571 average. "I'm hitting like a Yankee again," he gloated. He was the only one.

Beaten twice at home by two southpaws, we flew to California needing to win two out of three in the Dodgers' new playground in Chavez Ravine to keep the Series going. The Dodgers had their big, mean right-hander, Don Drysdale, waiting for us. We called on Jim Bouton.

The Dodgers did what they did best, they manufactured a run in the first inning on a walk to Gilliam, a wild pitch and a single by Tommy Davis that had some reverse English on it. The ball caromed off Richardson's shin and skidded into right field. Bouton was as stingy as Drysdale after that, but the damage was done. He held the Dodgers to four hits before Yogi hit for him in the eighth. In what turned out to be his only appearance in the Series, and the last at bat of his American League career, Berra lined out to Ron Fairly in right field.

For just an instant in the ninth, with two out and nobody on, it looked as if we might have a tie game. Joe Pepitone sent a fly ball to deep right that appeared headed for the Dodger bull pen. But Fairly backed up to the fence and made the catch for the last out.

Neither team had an extra base hit. Drysdale shut us out on three singles, striking out nine, four of them called. I had one of our hits, a bunt that bounced over Gilliam's head at third for a single. I was now 1 for 11 in the Series.

We were hitting .166 as a team. Did someone say slump? We had curled up like shrimp on a hot greased grill. We were staring at a sweep, an embarrassment that no Yankee team had suffered in the years I had worn pinstripes, and only once in this century, in 1922. They were swept by John McGraw's Giants, with all the games taking place at the Polo Grounds. The Yankees didn't have their own stadium yet. Their leading hitter that year was Wally Pipp, the first baseman whose job would be taken by Lou Gehrig.

So we were trying to avoid equaling a record of futility that had stood for forty-one years. It was going to be Koufax and Ford again in the fourth game, and we couldn't find anything so far that would give us any confidence. Whitey showed up at the ballpark with a bandage on his right index finger. Feeling around in his shaving kit, he had gashed the finger when it slid across the blade of his razor. "I don't know what made me reach with my right hand," he said to me, "but I'm sure glad I did. Imagine if I had done it to my left hand? Everyone would have said I did it on purpose."

Before we went on the field for Game 4, Ralph Houk reminded us: "No matter what happens out there today, we've had a great season."

Whitey pitched seven innings before Houk lifted him

for a pinch hitter. The Dodgers were held to just two hits, both by Frank Howard, the second a monster homer into the upper deck in left, above the 450-foot marker. The message board—the Dodgers were the first team to have a screen for messages and videos—said that no ball had been hit there before. Of course, Dodger Stadium was only two years old and there were a lot of places the ball hadn't been hit yet.

With Koufax on the mound, that one on the scoreboard looked like a big lead. His fastball wasn't as overpowering as in the first game, but his curve was giving us fits. He would strike out eight, walk none. With one out in the seventh, he threw me a fastball letter-high, and I stepped into it and tied the score with a homer into the pavilion in left-center. In our dugout, the whole team was standing and waiting to greet me when I crossed the plate.

We had come from behind to tie the score for the first time in thirty-four innings. The homer was my fifteenth in the World Series, tying Ruth's record. In less than thirty minutes, it was not going to seem like a very big deal.

The Dodgers scored the winning run in their half of the seventh without getting a base hit. Gilliam hit a high chopper to Clete Boyer, who had to leave his feet to get it. But Pepitone lost the ball in the background of white shirts in the box seats. The ball hit him on the wrist, bounced off his chest, and rolled to the fence. By the time he chased it down, Gilliam was standing on third.

A routine play had turned into a three-base error. Pepi was three days away from his twenty-third birthday. I knew how he felt; he wanted to crawl into a hole. He was a wise-ass kid, but he was still a kid.

The next hitter, Willie Davis, flied out to deep center. My throw made it to the plate on one bounce, but Gilliam scored and the Dodgers had regained the lead, 2-1.

We put the tying run on base in each of the last two innings. In the eighth, Phil Linz singled, but Koufax got Tony Kubek to hit into a double play. In the ninth, Bobby

Richardson led off with a single. Sandy got Tresh and me on called strikes, but Elston Howard reached base on an error by Tracewski. We still had a pulse, but Hector Lopez grounded to short and the Dodgers had won the World Series for Los Angeles for the second time.

Humiliated may be too harsh a word, but I can't express how embarrassed we were. The Dodgers certainly deserved to win, but what couldn't be explained was how feeble we were. This kind of pratfall didn't happen to the Yankees. We were not supposed to lose a World Series in four games. We had seen good pitching before, but never this good for four straight games. The Dodgers smothered us with Koufax, twice, Podres, and Drysdale.

The Yankees had scored four runs in thirty-six innings. We struck out thirty-seven times. We never led in any game and twice had been behind after one inning. These had been Death Valley days.

It was going to be a dry off-season, but not a dull one. A week after Yogi put his catcher's mitt away, the Yankees announced that Ralph Houk was being moved upstairs to general manager, and Berra would succeed him as the new manager.

I was happy for Yogi, if you think managing a baseball team is a good thing to have happen to you. I don't think you heard the word "communication" so much in 1963, but some people wondered if Yogi could give orders, if he would be taken seriously. I wasn't worried about his doing the job. He knew the game. He had been calling pitches all his life.

But no one on the club had any doubts about why the change was made. In two words, Casey Stengel. The attendance was dropping at Yankee Stadium. The front office wanted a warmer image to compete with the happy crowds that were flocking to see the Mets, the expansion team, the lovable underdogs.

# YOGI AND THE LAST HURRAH

## 1964—CARDINALS 4, YANKEES 3

Very few ball players are able to recognize the exact moment when their skills start slipping. Willie Pep, the old boxing champ, once said there were three ways to tell: "First, your legs go. Then your reflexes go. Then your friends go."

It isn't quite the same with a team, but it's close. The Yankees were slipping in 1964, but it was hard to tell because we won the pennant.

The off-season was more of a mixed bag than usual. I had surgery on my other knee, the left one, which leads to the obvious question: So what else was new? The big thing was knowing that Yogi would be the manager.

Lawrence Peter Berra it says in the *Baseball Encyclopedia* and I guess other official places, such as his birth certificate. I wanted to be healthy for him. I wanted to have a good year for him. We had been friends and teammates since the first day I met him, in spring training in 1951. I had a fear that the season might be a rough one and that managing might change him, so I tried not to dwell on such things. What I didn't expect was what a terrific year it would turn out to be, how he would pull the club together and lead us into the World Series, and then get fired.

But I'm getting ahead of myself. There are a few points I need to make about Yogi, before I get to the '64 Series and how it was overshadowed by all the intrigue that took place, before and after the games were played. As his friend, Yogi worried about me, about why I didn't pay more attention to the game, and how easy I was with my money.

I threw money around pretty good, as a reaction to growing up without any. Yogi's family was almost as poor as mine, but he had the other reaction. He tossed half-dollars around like they were manhole covers.

Yogi signed with the Yankees in the summer of 1942 for a bonus of $500. The money came hard and because of it he almost walked away from this dream he had of being a professional baseball player. Yogi was seventeen that summer, even then proud and stubborn. The year before, the St. Louis Cardinals had signed his best friend, Joe Garagiola, out of a try-out camp both attended. Both were catchers who batted left-handed. The Cards paid Garagiola $500 to sign. They offered Yogi a contract, but no bonus. All they saw was a kid with a squatty body and an odd gait. It almost killed him to do it, but he turned them down. "I wasn't jealous of Joey," he told me, even then his face clouding up, remembering this insult from his hometown team. "I was glad for him. But I knew I was worth it, too. I wasn't gonna play unless I got it. For one thing, I knew it was gonna be hard enough to talk my folks into letting me go."

He got his $500 from the Yankees, but they played some games with him. They took the bonus out of his take-home pay, so he was making $35 every two weeks and writing home to his mother for an extra ten-spot so he could eat.

He played that season for the Norfolk Tars, then joined the navy, saw action on an LST, was in the thick of the D-Day invasion, and came home with a bunch of medals. He was on leave from the navy when the Yankees invited him to the Stadium for a workout. He was dressed in that shapeless blue uniform with the bell bottoms and the middie blouse and the white cap cocked over one eye. The clubhouse man, Pete Sheehy, looked at him in disbelief when he asked for his gear.

Yogi shifted his weight uncomfortably and then said, "I guess I don't look like a ballplayer."

Pete shook his head. "You don't even look like a sailor," he said.

By 1946 he was home and appeared at the end of the season with the Yankees. Joe Garagiola was in the World Series that year with the Cardinals, and what were the odds that two kids from the same block would wind up catching for two big-league teams?

Years later, Garagiola practically invented a night club act around the fact that he and Yogi grew up together in St. Louis. The Berras lived at 5447 Elizabeth Avenue, the Garagiolas at 5446, on what was known as "Dago Hill." Joe would always get a laugh on the banquet circuit when he told his audience, with the air of a guy explaining something real complicated, "A lot of Italian families lived on that hill, you see, and that is the reason it was called Dago Hill."

His name appeared in a Yankee box score for the first time—it would show up in more than two thousand of them—in the second game of a doubleheader in late September of 1946. He caught nine innings against the Philadelphia Athletics. No one stole on him. He had a single and a homer and drove in two runs. The Yankees won, 4-3.

"Of considerable interest," wrote Harold Rosenthal in the *New York Herald-Tribune*, "was the appearance of several recent Yankee acquisitions. Bobby Brown, Newark's hard-hitting shortstop, made his debut as did Larry Berra, the Newark catcher."

The press figured he was a character, with his five-eight frame and his long arms and happy Halloween face. Actually, he was not yet either a character or a polished catcher. The Yankees assigned Bill Dickey to work with him, and later Yogi expressed his gratitude to Bill for "learning me all his experiences." Dickey helped make him a catcher and his tangled way with words made him a character.

For most of our careers, neither one of us liked to go to a banquet and have to get up and speak. I improved some, I hope, but Yogi once confided to me that he never got over being terrified when he stood in front of an audience. I asked him what happened when he didn't start firing a barrage of one-liners and jokes at them?

He said, "They act surprised."

I said, "Then what do you do?"

"I tell them to ask me questions. But the funny thing is, sometimes I just stand there and they start laughing."

I always thought it was curious, the image people had of him. He never talked much and he wasn't a slapstick kind of guy. When it came to baseball, he was smart as tear gas. Not book smart or in some educated or calculating way. Street smart, people smart.

But he said maybe a third of what he has been quoted as saying. Garagiola made up a third and the writers made up the rest. In more than a few ways, Yogi was like Casey Stengel. They both had the kind of face that was ageless— them and George Burns. I mean, they would look about as good at ninety as they did at nineteen. Neither one was a worrier. They were both basically secretive. Stengel would hide his opinions in a torrent of words. Yogi would just shut up. He was a man of long silences and his wit was accidental.

If you took the time, you could see that what each of

them said usually made a lot of sense. Of course, not everybody had that much time.

It was after a World Series game that Yogi was introduced to Ernest Hemingway at a party at Toots Shor's. When he returned to the table where some of the Yankees were sitting, he was asked what he thought of Hemingway. "He's quite a character," said Berra. "What does he do?"

"Well, he's a writer," Hank Bauer said.

"Is that so?" said Yogi. "Which paper?"

That's funny, but it didn't prove anything. A lot of guys in sports spend their lives in a thimble. Many years later, Joe Gibbs, the coach of the Washington Redskins football team, was interviewed before a Super Bowl game. Somebody made a reference to Madonna. Gibbs said he had never heard of her.

Berra was qualified to run a baseball team and Stengel saw right away that Yogi would be his eyes on the field. He would refer to him as, "Mr. Berra, which is my assistant manager."

In a roundabout way, Casey was responsible for Yogi getting his shot.

I didn't see Casey during the season, of course, but I would talk to him now and then on the phone, bump into him on occasion in a restaurant or a charity dinner. Most of all, I read about him in the papers and it was great. It was killing the Yankees' top brass that Stengel and Weiss—who followed Casey to the Mets when the Yankees retired him—were somehow winning a war for the minds and hearts of the fans of New York. And they were doing it with a last-place team.

Casey had been bitter about the way he was replaced, and for a short while I think that affected how he felt about Ralph Houk. That's human nature. At the same time, some of the players thought that in order to be loyal to Houk and the club they had to knock Casey. That's human nature, too.

I remember the day they announced that Casey was "retiring," and there were references to a youth movement on the club. With disdain, Stengel had told the press, "Youth is for kids."

Then, suddenly, he was the manager of the new team in New York and even before they signed their first player he called them, "the amazing Mets." The rookies they signed were "the youth of America," and he would say things like: "Look how big it is, the youth of America. Every day they set a new record."

He was including guys in track and swimmers and pro football players. From what I could tell, he hadn't changed much. I'd catch some of their games on television, and when the cameras cut to the Mets' dugout, as they often did, I'd see Casey hunched over like a guy who has been repairing watches all his life. But when he moved, he moved in spurts like an old movie. He skipped a lot and clapped his hands a lot, the way kids do. And he could still be brutally honest. The Mets were expected to be better their second year, and when they were beaten on opening day, Casey said, "The attendance was robbed. We're still a fraud."

Yogi kept up with him, too. "Casey tries to get you mad," he said. "I argued with him once and then went out and got three hits. Afterwards, he called me into his office and said, 'See, I got you mad.' He never kept anything in. He always let it out. Maybe that's why he lasted so long."

In the spring, somebody asked Berra to explain Casey's success over so many years with the Yankees. "Well," he said, with simple logic, "he had some very good players."

We heard about Stengel from the writers who moved from camp to camp in Florida. The Yankees had moved to Fort Lauderdale, and the Mets were now in St. Petersburg, where Casey had showed up with his hair dyed a strange, youthful shade of henna. It was a wild sight, they said, and I imagine it was, with that hair and that wrinkled, almost biblical face. The writers could hardly wait to tell you about him.

"Have you seen Casey?" one of them greeted me. "He looks like Dorian Grey's uncle." The reference was to a short story about a guy who never aged, but whose portrait in the attic changed and grew more frightening to look at with each sinful act of his life.

So as we headed north to open the 1964 season, we were competing with ten teams in the American League and one grumpy but beautiful old man in New York.

By June we were in third place, behind the Orioles and the White Sox, and there was already a good deal of grumbling about Berra's managing. But like Houk the previous year, he had to do a lot of juggling because we were riddled with injuries. At one point, the whole starting outfield was on the bench with pulled hamstring muscles.

The Yankees made two moves in the second half that firmed up our pitching. We brought up rookie Mel Stottlemyre from Richmond in August, and acquired Pedro Ramos, a fine relief pitcher, from the Indians, in September. Our walking wounded got well, we won eleven straight, and finished strong to win our fifth pennant in a row.

That good stretch run reminded me of the Yankees of old. In a game against the Angels, I picked up my two-thousandth hit, joining Ruth, Gehrig, DiMaggio, and Berra as the fifth Yankee in that elite group. The season marked something of a comeback for me. I played in 143 games and hit .303, with 35 homers and 111 runs batted in. But my legs were still wobbly, and Maris played most of the season in center field. I moved between left and right.

I don't believe anyone could have done a better job of managing that year than Yogi. It wasn't easy because he had to contend with the presence in the front office of Houk, to whom authority came naturally. The players were fond of Berra, but they didn't fear him.

He could analyze things better than he could explain or

describe them. It was easy to misunderstand him. I pulled a thigh muscle one day running to first, and as I limped into the dugout Yogi was concerned. He said, "What's the matter with YOU?" The emphasis was on the word "you," which made it sound sarcastic, not at all what he meant. To the newer players it sounded awful and some of them were irritated. They were thinking, "This is the Mick. Why is Yogi putting him down?" It just came out wrong. Yogi really wanted to know where I was hurt. When the pain subsided, I had to walk around and clear the air for him.

Yogi gained their respect gradually over the season, as they saw how often he called the right pitch, the right play, and made the right estimate of a player's ability. The club was drifting when we picked up Ramos in early September to fill a gaping hole in the bull pen.

"He can pitch every day," one of our scouts said.

"He's going to have to," said Berra, and that was how he used him. He helped get us there, but because we traded for him after the first of September he wasn't on our roster for the World Series.

I'm not trying to brag, but in a way, unintentionally, I may have turned the team around for Yogi. In the middle of the race, in late August, we had just lost four straight to the White Sox, including both halves of a doubleheader. The bus ride from Comiskey Park to O'Hare Airport was a quiet one. Linz, who was in the back of the bus, pulled out a harmonica he was learning to play and softly tooted "Mary Had a Little Lamb," the only song he knew. Berra turned around and shouted toward the back, "Shove that thing up your ass!"

Linz didn't hear him, so he asked me what the manager had said. I told him, "He said, if you're gonna play that thing, play it faster."

Which Phil did. Now Berra stormed to the back of the bus and knocked the harmonica out of his hand. The instrument hit Joe Pepitone on the knee, and Pepi let out a yelp in mock pain. Soon everybody but Yogi was laughing.

After Berra returned to his seat, I retrieved the harmonica and said to Whitey, who was sitting across the aisle, "It looks like I'm going to be managing this club pretty soon. You can be my third-base coach. And here's what we'll do. One toot, that's a bunt. Two toots, that's a hit and run."

Linz was fined $200. He also got a $20,000 endorsement contract from a harmonica company.

It may have been a coincidence, but from then on the players seemed to have more respect for Berra. They had seen his temper and they believed he had drawn a line. We played some of our best ball the rest of the season. The stories began to dry up about the players taking advantage of Berra's sweet nature.

Of course, that club would have been a test for anybody. It had such free spirits as Linz, Pepitone, and Jim Bouton—not to mention Whitey and me. Yogi had named Ford his pitching coach, and we were the team's senior citizens, but what the heck, we still broke a few curfews.

We won the pennant by a game over the White Sox and two in front of the Orioles. Our race was exciting, but the one in the National League was a fan's dream. Four clubs were in the race at the wire—the Phillies, Reds, Giants, and Cardinals—and at one time or another each of them had been counted out. The Phillies lost ten in a row and blew a lead of six and a half games with twelve to play. It was one of the steepest dives in baseball history. "It was like watching someone drown," said Gene Mauch, their manager.

Gus Triandos, the Phillies' catcher, called it, "The year of the blue snow."

Meanwhile, the Reds were gallantly trying to win the flag for their manager, Fred Hutchinson, who was dying of cancer, and who gave up the team to Dick Sisler in August. Sisler was called the "acting manager," a phrase with a reassuring, temporary ring to it. But the Reds would never again jump to the orders of Fred Hutchinson. He knew it and they knew it. He would be dead in November.

I had batted against Hutch when he was a pitcher for

the Tigers. He was a terrific competitor. The teams that followed the Tigers into Yankee Stadium could tell how Hutch had done by the number of chairs and light bulbs that had been smashed in the visitor's clubhouse.

The Giants were the first of the final four to drop out. The Cardinals, under a good company man named Johnny Keane, won eight in a row to leap past the Phillies and Reds into first place. Then they lost two out of three to the comical Mets, then won the pennant on the final day.

The Cardinals not only surprised the Phillies, the Reds, and the experts. They surprised their ownership. Bing Devine, the team's general manager and Johnny Keane's best friend, had been fired in August with the club in third place. The papers were saying the manager's job had been offered to Leo Durocher, effective the end of the season. Keane heard the rumors and kept his silence.

Man, talk about a public relations problem. The Cards had a beauty on their hands. When the club rallied and won the pennant, the offer to Leo was withdrawn and Augie Busch offered Keane a new contract. He left them dangling, said he would talk about it after the World Series.

We followed the race in the other league, curious about which team we'd play in October. But we knew little of what was going on behind the scenes and, in any case, would not have suspected that it would effect us and the Yankee tradition. That was where matters stood when the 1964 World Series opened in St. Louis. We were hurting again. Tony Kubek was out with a sprained wrist, with Phil Linz replacing him at short.

The Cardinals looked to us like a patchwork team, but it worked for them on the field. They had speed at the top of the order in Curt Flood and Lou Brock, a young outfielder they had gotten from the Cubs for pitcher Ernie Broglio—in what would turn out to be one of the most lopsided trades ever made. They had some power in Bill White and Ken Boyer, Clete's older brother. Dick Groat, the ex-Pirate, was past his prime at short, but he gave them leadership. A rookie, Tim McCarver, was behind the plate.

Their top pitchers were Bob Gibson, Ray Sadecki, and Curt Simmons, the left-hander who had been cast off by the Phillies. The Cards had brought up Barney Schultz, a thirty-eight-year-old knuckleball pitcher, from the minors in August. With that cast, the club had made it back to the World Series for the first time since 1946. I had listened to that Series on the radio in the hospital in Oklahoma City, while the doctors tried to save my leg from osteomyelitis. The Cardinals had been my boyhood team. This encounter kind of closed a circle for me and way back in my mind, I realized it.

This was going to be a Series with a lot of angles, some sharper than others. The Boyers were starting at third base for each team, and that may have been the first time brothers opposed each other at the same position in the World Series.

Whitey Ford started for us—who else?—against their young right-hander, Ray Sadecki, a twenty-game winner. Whitey was pitching with a sore arm, and it was not going to improve as the game went on. He gave up runs to the Cards in the first two innings, and my throwing error let in the second. I was playing in right to take the strain off my legs and then I wind up costing us a run with my arm for Pete's sake.

But Tom Tresh pumped a two-run homer into the seats in left-center in the second inning, and after five we led, 4-2. I singled and scored the fourth run when Tresh doubled over third base. Tom was off to a fast start.

Then in the sixth, Ford's arm gave out and he would not pitch in an another World Series game, not that week, not ever again. After Ken Boyer singled, Mike Shannon hit a booming homer that just missed the "B" in the Budweiser sign atop the scoreboard in left. McCarver doubled. Lefty Al Downing replaced Whitey. A single by Carl Warwick, pinch-hitting for Sadecki, and Curt Flood's triple scored two more.

In the eighth, with Barney Schultz pitching, Yogi sent up John Blanchard to swing for Downing and he doubled into the right-field corner, then came home on a single by Bobby Richardson. We had cut the lead to 6-5. The inning before, I hit a knuckleball off the screen in right for a single. That's how bad my legs were. I could only get a single out of it.

The Cardinals iced the game with three more in the last of the eighth on an error, a walk, an intentional walk, Flood's single, and a double by Brock. Yogi went to the bull pen three times for Downing, Rollie Sheldon, and Pete Mikkelsen. The final score was 9-5.

The writers asked Berra a really dumb question: Did he wish he had Pedro Ramos out there? Yogi swallowed a bite of his ham sandwich and then laughed. "But we don't have him," he said.

Ramos was back in New York. The Yankees, always thinking so far ahead in the past, had made the trade a few days too late to qualify him for the Series.

One of the St. Louis heroes was ole Barney Schultz, who pitched the last three innings, gave up the run in the eighth, and retired us in order in the ninth. Some story. He had pitched eighteen years in the minors, in places like Wilmington, Terre Haute, Schenectady, Macon, Des Moines, Hollywood, Houston. He had a lot of years to think about what he would do if he ever got in a World Series. He was at Jacksonville, Florida, when the Cardinals called him up on the first of August. He saved eleven games for them the last two months and had an earned run average of 1.65.

Johnny Keane had bounced around the minors as a manager even longer. Their paths crossed more than once.

Whitey didn't tell anyone yet that he had reinjured his arm. He just said, "It's a little easier pitching in New York. You can make a mistake there and it's just a fly ball." Busch Stadium was a small park and the wind was blowing out.

With Sadecki coming through in the opener, Keane now had his big gun, Gibson, and the veteran Simmons ready for us. Yogi went with Mel Stottlemyre in Game 2, and he ended our five-game losing streak, dating back to last year's sweep by the Dodgers.

They won it fairly big, 8-3, but the score was tied for five innings and the turning point was a play the Cardinals questioned. I was on base with a walk and one out in the sixth, when Joe Pepitone was hit on the thigh. That moved me into scoring position and Tresh drove me across with a single. We were up a run and added two in the seventh. Phil Linz led off the ninth with his first and only World Series homer and that started a final, four-run rally. Maris singled, I doubled, Pepi singled, and Tresh hit a sacrifice fly.

But both clubs seemed to agree that Pepitone getting hit on the thigh changed the game because it led to the go-ahead run. The Cardinals argued that the ball clipped his bat first. Keane said, "It may have hit him, but we heard it hit the bat first. Tim McCarver saw it, Gibson saw it, our whole bench saw it."

Umpire Bill McKinley disagreed. "Pepitone took a sort of half swing," said Bill, "but he didn't hit it. The curve ball came in and hit him right there," and he pointed to his right thigh.

In our clubhouse, Pepi said the ball plunked him on the left thigh, and he dropped his pants to show off a slight redness. "That's the thigh," he said. "See it? It didn't hurt, but it stung. Right there."

Just having Pepitone stand there in the middle of the clubhouse, with his pants down and all those writers surrounding him, was enough to make the game special.

I called my shot in Game 3 and hit a home run in the ninth to beat the Cardinals and Barney Schultz. I acted out of frustation, not showmanship. I had mishandled a base hit by Tim McCarver in the fifth and that error led to the tying run for St. Louis.

The Series had moved to Yankee Stadium and the score

was 1-1 through eight innings of a terrific pitcher's duel between Jim Bouton and Curt Simmons. I almost had another muff in the top of the ninth, when I misjudged Curt Flood's liner and almost stumbled making the catch.

I was angry when I headed for the plate in the bottom of the ninth. I passed Elston Howard in the on-deck circle and said, "You might as well go on in. I'm gonna hit the first pitch I see out of the park."

It happened just about that way. The Cardinals had pinch-hit for Simmons and Schultz came in to pitch the ninth—and face one batter, as it turned out. I took a rip at his first pitch and I knew instantly the ball was gone. It landed in the third deck of the right field; another few feet and it would have cleared the roof. The game was over, 2-1.

Frank Crosetti, our third-base coach, followed me down the line, beating me on the back, and a whole crowd of Yankees waited for me at home plate. They were telling each other what I had said to Ellie, and loving it.

The homer was my sixteenth in World Series play, breaking Babe Ruth's record. I would add two more against the Cardinals for a total of eighteen, and that is a record I expect to keep. I doubt anyone else will ever get to appear in twelve World Series in fourteen years. I was so elated, I posed for the photographers in the clubhouse hugging Bouton, who wasn't real popular with his teammates even before he wrote his best-selling book, *Ball Four*. By today's standard, the book is pretty tame and the truth is, I didn't dislike Jim. He was different, all right, a maverick. He cared about the game, but he didn't seem to take anything seriously.

That side of him didn't bother me. When Bouton won his first big league start against the Senators, I was the one who laid down a path of white towels leading to his locker. I kind of went along with the guys on Bouton, but if he had joined the Yankees earlier, before I was on my last legs, we might have been friends.

The thing is, when his book came out it violated the

code that had existed among players for nearly a century. It can be summed up in the words of a sign that hung in the clubhouse: WHAT IS SAID HERE, STAYS HERE. Outside the white lines we believed our business was nobody else's business. If the players resented the press for digging into our private lives, how were we supposed to feel when a teammate did it?

Anyway, Bouton pitched great, allowing six hits, five of them singles, striking out three, and walking none. The photograph of me and Bouton hangs on the wall of the trophy room Merlyn designed for our house in Dallas. If she had known at the time who the other guy was in the picture, I think she would have tossed it in the can.

I have to admit, that was an unforgettable game for me. All fans enjoy those clap-of-thunder endings and I'm a fan. The writers lapped it up. I was described as "the majestic invalid," and even with my limp they said I "cantered" around the bases.

The Yankees were up two games to one, and we would have felt real cocky going into Game 4 except that we had lost Whitey. Al Downing started against Sadecki and we gave him a three-run lead in the first inning. Phil Linz doubled to open the inning, tried to steal third, got caught in a rundown, and was safe on Ken Boyer's throwing error. Then Richardson doubled, stopped at third on a hit by Maris, and scored on my single. I was out trying to stretch it into two bases, and with Maris at third the Cards changed pitchers.

Sadecki was lifted for Roger Craig, the ex-Dodger and former twenty-game loser with Casey Stengel's Mets. Howard's single scored the third run. We sure as hell didn't figure that Craig and Ron Taylor would shut us out the last eight innings.

But they did, and in the sixth, the Cardinals loaded the bases on singles by Warwick and Flood and an error by Richardson on Dick Groat's grounder. Then Ken Boyer cleared them, stepping into a high change-up by Downing, and ripping the ball into the left-field stands. It was the ninth grand-slam homer in the history of the World Series, and the Cardinals won, 4-3, with all the scoring limited to two innings.

K. Boyer, as he was known in the box score, said: "When I rounded third I was kind of looking for Clete to say something. He didn't say a word, and I didn't think it was my place to say anything. I looked right at him and he had a sort of puzzled look on his face."

Taylor, a tall Canadian right-hander, retired the first eight batters to face him and allowed just one runner in the final four innings. I walked on a full count in the eighth with two down, but Taylor struck out Elston.

This was turning into one hellacious Series. Tim McCarver, a kid the Yankees had tried hard to sign, hit a three-run homer in the tenth inning of Game 5 to carry the Cardinals to a 5-2 victory. In the last of the ninth, Tom Tresh had tied it with a two-out, two-run homer off Bob Gibson, who went all the way.

Gibson was a terrific athlete, a basketball star at Creighton and, briefly, a Harlem Globetrotter. He stopped us cold for eight innings, and he showed us his catlike quickness in the ninth. I led off the inning and dribbled a grounder to short. When Groat bobbled the ball for an error, I beat the throw to first. Then Pepitone slashed a line drive off Gibson's hip and bounced toward third. The pitcher raced after it, turned and threw to first to get Pepi by an eyelash. Yogi and Joe and three or four other Yankees argued the call, so we had one runner on base instead of two when Tresh unloaded on the next pitch for a homer that tied the score.

And McCarver, having a sensational Series, untied it off Pete Mikkelsen, after a walk to Bill White and a bunt single by Ken Boyer put runners at first and third.

Johnny Keane had started to give McCarver the signal to lay down a squeeze bunt, but he saw Elston Howard staring at him. "He had been watching me the whole game," said Keane, "and I thought he had guessed what we were up to, so we let Tim hit."

McCarver was four days away from his twenty-third birthday. He was giddy after the game and I knew how he felt. "I didn't think it was a home run," he said. "But I saw Mickey Mantle going back and I felt good because I knew at least it would get White home. I saw the ball go in the stands as I neared first, but I couldn't believe it. By the time I got to third I was laughing out loud. I'm always laughing, you know, even when I'm sad. The way I feel now, I'll never be sad again." The Cards were ahead, three games to two.

"Meet me in St. Louis" was the phrase that took us to the sixth game, with the Yankees needing another big effort from Jim Bouton against Curt Simmons. We got one, but this time we backed it up with some old-time Yankee lightning.

With the score 1-1 in the top of the sixth, Roger Maris and I homered on successive pitches. I don't think we had done that since 1961. It was the fourth time teammates had done it in the World Series. Ruth and Gehrig connected in 1928 and again in '32. Roger hit his just inside the right-field foul pole. I hit mine onto the roof of the right-field pavilion, my seventeenth in the World Series, and we led, 3-1.

Before the Cardinals could recover from that combination, Joe Pepitone slugged a grand-slam homer off Gordon Richardson, who had just come into the game in the eighth. This one was on the right-field roof, too.

Bouton pitched in and out of trouble all day and was dog tired by the ninth. Steve Hamilton came in to give up a run-scoring single, then get Curt Flood on a game-ending double play as the Yankees evened the Series, 8-3.

For the eighth time in my career, we were going to the seventh game, a one-day season, winner take all. Yogi went with Mel Stottlemyre against Gibson, who was pitching for the third time in five games. The Cardinals staked him to a seven-run lead before we could mount a comeback and put any suspense in the game. They scored three runs each in the fourth and fifth, knocking out Stottlemyre on two singles, a walk, an error, and a double steal.

They continued the assault on Al Downing, with Lou Brock drilling a homer off the roof in right-center and a single, a double, and a sacrifice fly bringing in the last two. It was 6-0, with Gibson in command, and in the stands the St. Louis fans started celebrating.

I'm proud of the fact that we didn't roll over. I didn't know this would be my last World Series game, but at least I went out with a home run, my eighteenth. Richardson beat out a roller and Maris singled to right. He threw me a high hard one that may have been outside the strike zone, but I reached for the ball and poked it to the opposite field for a three-run homer.

That trimmed the score to 6-3 and Gibson was annoyed. He shook his head later and said, "That man has power."

The Cardinals took one of the runs back on Ken Boyer's solo homer in the seventh off Hamilton, the fourth of five pitchers used by Berra. In the ninth, Gibson gave up homers with the bases empty to Phil Linz and Clete Boyer, and Keane went to the mound, he explained later, "to look into his face and see if he still had that determined look."

Apparently, he did. Richardson popped out to second and the Cards had won, 7-5, and in the clubhouse the Yankees were playing the what-if game. "If Richardson gets on in the ninth," said Yogi, "with Maris and Mantle coming up, I think he would have been taken out." It was as if getting rid of Gibson equaled a win. Maybe so.

Stottlemyre hurt his shoulder in the fourth, when he covered first on a double play attempt and had to dive for a low throw from Linz. The game was scoreless up to then, but his arm stiffened and Yogi replaced him an inning later.

"If Whitey had been available," said Yogi, "he would

have been in there." But Ford had hurt his arm in the first game, and never reappeared.

As the saying goes, "If Ifs and Buts were candy and nuts, we'd all have a Merry Christmas."

I had my best World Series in years. I batted .333, hit three homers, scored eight runs, drove in eight, and established career records for homers, runs, RBI, walks, extra base hits, and total bases. But none of it counted for much then. We lost.

And now the real explosion came. The next morning, a Friday, Johnny Keane met with Augie Busch, the owner of the Cardinals, to talk about his new contract. They didn't talk long. Keane turned it down. He handed Busch his letter of resignation when he walked into the room.

Back in early September, when the Cards didn't seem on the verge of winning anything, Busch and his advisers decided they needed a new manager and they lined up Durocher. Keane had worked thirty-four years in the St. Louis organization. He had been a prospect as a shortstop, but a pitcher named Sig Jakucki stuck one in his ear and when Keane woke up seven days later his playing days were over.

Jakucki was a shipyard worker in the mid-forties during the war, when teams were desperate for players. The St. Louis Browns offered him a contract, and he pitched in the 1944 World Series against the Cardinals.

Keane became a manager, who won wherever he went. He first interviewed for the Cardinal job in 1950 and seemed to have it locked up. But Marty Marion was hired out of nowhere and Keane went back to the farms. Keane was passed over for Eddie Stanky in 1952, for Harry Walker in 1955, Fred Hutchinson in 1956, and for Solly Hemus, one of his former minor league players, in 1957. You can figure out from this list that (a) the Cardinals were firing a lot of managers, and (b) Johnny Keane had a very high pain threshhold.

He accepted a job on Hemus's staff and then replaced him in 1961. He took a bad team and finished fifth, sixth, second, and first, and while he was winning it his bosses were hiring another guy.

Like the fans and the press, the Yankee players were fascinated by this melodrama for a long time, maybe half a day. First came the news that Keane had quit, and at about the same time the Yankees called a press conference and announced that Yogi had been fired as manager, but would stay in the organization as a "field consultant" to Ralph Houk. I guess that was a better title than "vice president in charge of staying in touch."

Houk said the decision was made before the World Series and Yogi was given the news that Friday morning. Yogi reacted predictably. He said, "I don't mind. At least, I'll be spending the year at home. Where else can you get a job like this?" His home was in Montclair, New Jersey. He had hit 358 homers in his 17 years with the club, and played in more games than any Yankee except Lou Gehrig.

The Yankee players were shocked. Busch described himself as "stunned." Keane had told him not to make an offer, his decision was firm. "I didn't want to embarrass him," he said, "but no offer was acceptable." Keane said he didn't have another job, but he wouldn't be without one long.

We could all see what was coming next, big as a curveball that doesn't break and floats in letter-high. On Tuesday, the Yankees announced that Johnny Keane would be their fourth manager in six years. Even though we had won the pennant, the front office decided that the club lacked discipline, and Yogi would not be able to provide it. Keane would.

Maybe he did, but he was totally wrong for the Yankees. Keane was a quiet and decent man, but aloof and a believer in keeping his distance from the players. He had a need, I think, to show his authority by putting me in my place, and he never seemed to accept the idea that when I couldn't play I was truly hurting.

His timing was awful. He caught the Yankees on their

downward slide, and he did nothing to delay it. We fell to sixth his first season. The club was in last place in 1966 when the Yankees fired him and restored Ralph Houk to the manager's chair, proving again that in baseball, as in war and politics, there are no final victories.

"The dumbest thing the Yankees ever did," said Whitey, "was fire Yogi Berra. They had to wait another twelve years before they could get back to another World Series."

The last years of my career were a blur. Yogi went over to the Mets in 1965 and Casey talked him into coming out of retirement for part of the season. Then one night Tony Cloninger of the Braves struck him out three times, all on fastballs, and Yogi decided on the spot to retire and stay that way. He never kidded himself.

Late in my career, when I had a face that people knew, I foolishly said to my teammates that I wondered how it would feel to have a season when there was no pressure on me. Every year, it seemed, I would be in contention for the home run title, or expected to lead the Yankees to the World Series. I would be talking to the press while my teammates were discussing where to have dinner. Well, I found out in 1966 how it would feel when we finished last.

Yet even as the years grew lean, I became aware that my place in the game, the image people had of me, had taken on a kind of permanence.

After one World Series, I went with a friend to take in a football game between the University of Texas and Texas Christian University in Fort Worth. On our way out of the stadium, we stopped by the locker room to say hello to the Texas coach, Darrell Royal. We shook hands and he could not have been nicer, saying how pleased he was to meet me.

I grinned and ducked my head and said, "Darrell, we've met before."

He looked puzzled and a little embarrassed. "We have?" He asked. "When was that?"

When I was a senior in high school, I told him, Bud

Wilkinson tried to recruit me to play football for Oklahoma. Royal was the quarterback, and he was the one Coach Wilkinson picked to show me around the campus.

"Oh, well," said Darrell, with a smile, "you weren't MIcky Mantle then."

By 1967, I needed that reminder. Everybody was gone. The Yankees made Whitey a scout, and I spent more of my time in my hotel room, ordering room service and feeling alone. The club moved me to first base to try and get another year out of my legs. I was part of an anonymous infield that included Horace Clarke at second base, Ruben Amaro at shortstop, and Charley Smith at third. I retired after the '68 season, declining in numbers and advancing in years.

The nineteen-year-old phenom was about to turn thirty-seven, and he knew it was time to leave. I knew there wouldn't be another World Series in my future and I was tired of settling for less.

# EPILOGUE

This is a book about the World Series, and the dozen I played in, and what that excitement and those times were like. There is no connection with what I feel I have to write about now, except for this: Winning the World Series, or even getting there, was a good reason for baseball players to celebrate. In my day, that usually meant a party, winding up at a nightclub or a restaurant or at the bar of a nice hotel. We might have come up short a few runs, but there was never a shortage of alcohol.

And so, more than forty years after I played in my first World Series, I checked into a treatment center in January 1994 to win the biggest game of my life. It took me a long while to realize I had become an alcoholic, longer to admit it.

I'm not ashamed to say that I have a drinking problem. It became more of a problem after I retired in 1969 and a lot worse the last ten years. It's an illness, in some cases a sneaky one, but like any illness, it can be treated. I am embarrassed that I didn't deal sooner with this weakness, and at the idea that I may have let down my fans, especially the young ones, the Little Leaguers.

But the Postal Service brought me sacks and sacks of mail from fans of mine who are now elderly, and from the kids, rooting for me, giving me support, some telling me they were proud that I had the courage to take the step I did.

I don't know that it took any courage, but it did take some common sense. I'm sober as I write this. I feel better than I have in years. My friends tell me I look great. I lost ten pounds. I'm eating more carefully, as opposed to some days when I didn't eat anything. I want to be well, and healthy, so I can stay around and enjoy all my friends and family.

But a point needs to be made about what damage the drinking did over the years. First, it made many days and nights difficult for the people who care about me the most. I wish I had been a better dad to my sons. And there is no doubt in my mind that alcohol hurt my career terribly. In the end, all you really have are the memories and the numbers on paper. The numbers are important because baseball is built on them, and this is the way you are measured.

And the point is, I played in more than 2,400 games, more than any Yankee player in history, and I hit 536 home runs, and I shouldn't be griping about my career. But I know it should have been so much better, and the big reason it wasn't is the lifestyle I chose, the late nights and too many empty glasses.

People always used to ask, "Who was better? Willie, Mickey, or Duke?" I've given the same answer before—the final stats say Willie was far ahead of us—but I never said why.

The fact is, Willie was one of the players who took care of himself, who really understood his body. And I can tell you, the mind may play games but the body never lies. All the great ones, such as Mays, Hank Aaron, Stan Musial, Ted Williams, and Joe DiMaggio, and I'm leaving out a bunch, had long careers and rose to the top of the record books.

I played eighteen years, but if I had gotten more rest, worked out more, lived a drier life, I might not have been injured as much. I didn't lose my enthusiasm for the game, I just lost the ability to do the things I used to do. I could have played a few more seasons if I had just taken my injuries more seriously. I'm not sure if I was lazy or didn't know better, but I didn't go to the trouble of doing the rehab on my leg as I was supposed to do.

I've never done drugs in my life, and I didn't really think about alcohol being addictive. I didn't give it much thought, period. I never took a drink until I joined the Yankees as a rookie in 1951. In those years, nobody used the phrase "substance abuse," certainly not in sports.

We traveled by train during most of the fifties, and there was always beer and alcohol on board, as there would be on the airline flights we would take later. But a plane gets you there in hours, a train could take all day or longer. There was plenty of time to talk baseball and satisfy whatever thirst you had. And we did. It all started out very innocently. That was baseball. That was part of what they call "male bonding" today.

The turning point for me was when my dad died of Hodgkin's disease during my second season with the Yankees. He was barely forty-one. If he had lived longer, I don't think the problem would have gone as far as it did. I couldn't have faced my dad if he knew I was drinking. When I lost him, I didn't have anyone to answer to except Casey Stengel, and the truth is he could outdrink most of his players.

You don't become an alcoholic overnight and, of course, you don't get well overnight, either. When I would head for the bright lights with Billy Martin and Whitey Ford, it was just a way of life on every team I knew about. I don't want that to sound like the three of us were the only ones going out on the town. There were not many on the club who didn't drink.

I'm not blaming baseball, or my teammates, or the travel, or the pain in my legs. The choices were mine to make. Even then I knew I had to draw a line. I grew up on stories of Babe Ruth going straight to the park after an all-night party, and then hitting two homers. I didn't make a habit of getting wasted the night before a game and going to the stadium with a hangover. I didn't want to feel I was hurting the team.

It was different with All-Star Games. Those were a three-day party for a lot of us and I will admit, I can barely remember some of them. Don Drysdale, Harvey Kuenn, and myself, the guys who were there every year, we just had a blast. Don and Harvey are both gone now. That may tell me something.

After I retired in 1969, my drinking got steadily worse. I can see it now. I have always been proud of the fact that all my life I have tried to be honest with people. I wish I had been more honest with myself. It hardly seems possible that I played my last game twenty-five years ago. But I did, and I missed the action, and I was bored. I started going to a lot of banquets and cocktail parties, and the drinking came easy. The next day someone might call and ask if I could remember what I had said to someone. And sometimes I couldn't.

And yet, right up until the last year, I didn't believe I was an alcoholic. I always thought I could take it or leave it.

What happened is, I needed surgery to replace the joints in both knees. And my doctor said he couldn't operate on me because my blood levels were so low, and my liver was almost ready to quit on me. After one exam, he looked me in the eye and said, "Mickey, the next drink you take might kill you."

I played golf with another doctor at Preston Trails in Dallas, and he pleaded with me to get help. He could look at me and see what shape I was in. That got my attention.

I knew then that I had to do something. I talked to my son Danny and to Pat Summerall, who had played football for the New York Giants when I was with the Yankees, and then had more success as a sportscaster. Both had been through this, had been through the clinic, and they encouraged me.

I can't do my career over and I can't get back the seasons I may have lost. But I am taking a fresh swing at life now and I am taking it cold sober. I do worry about the young people who have looked up to me. And I appeal to them: the best time not to do drugs or alcohol is the first time. Don't end up over the hill before you even start to climb it.

Mickey Mantle
Dallas, Texas
February 1994

# APPENDIXES

# YEAR-BY-YEAR STATS

## MICKEY CHARLES MANTLE
(The Commerce Comet)
b. Oct. 20, 1931, Spavinaw, Oklahoma
Hall of Fame, 1974

| Year | Club | G | B | R | H | HR | RBI | BA |
|------|------|-----|------|------|------|------|------|------|
| 1949 | Independence | 89 | 323 | 54 | 101 | 7 | 63 | .313 |
| 1950 | Joplin | 137 | 519 | *141 | *199 | 26 | 136 | .383 |
| 1951 | New York | 96 | 341 | 61 | 91 | 13 | 65 | .267 |
|      | Kansas City | 40 | 166 | 32 | 60 | 11 | 50 | .361 |
| 1952 | New York | 142 | 549 | 94 | 171 | 23 | 87 | .311 |
| 1953 | New York | 127 | 461 | 105 | 136 | 21 | 92 | .295 |
| 1954 | New York | 146 | 543 | *129 | 163 | 27 | 102 | .300 |
| 1955 | New York | 147 | 517 | 121 | 158 | *37 | 99 | .306 |
| 1956 | New York | 150 | 533 | *132 | 188 | *52 | *130 | *.353 |
| 1957 | New York | 144 | 474 | *121 | 173 | 34 | 94 | .365 |
| 1958 | New York | 150 | 519 | *127 | 158 | *42 | 97 | .304 |
| 1959 | New York | 144 | 541 | 104 | 154 | 31 | 75 | .285 |
| 1960 | New York | 153 | 527 | *119 | 145 | *40 | 94 | .275 |
| 1961 | New York | 153 | 514 | *132 | 163 | 54 | 128 | .317 |
| 1962 | New York | 123 | 377 | 96 | 121 | 30 | 89 | .321 |
| 1963 | New York | 65 | 172 | 40 | 54 | 15 | 35 | .314 |
| 1964 | New York | 143 | 465 | 92 | 141 | 35 | 111 | .303 |
| 1965 | New York | 122 | 361 | 44 | 92 | 19 | 46 | .255 |
| 1966 | New York | 108 | 333 | 40 | 96 | 23 | 56 | .288 |
| 1967 | New York | 144 | 440 | 63 | 108 | 22 | 55 | .245 |
| 1968 | New York | 144 | 435 | 57 | 103 | 18 | 54 | .237 |
| M.L. | Totals | 2401 | 8102 | 1677 | 2415 | 536 | 1509 | .298 |

| Year | Club | WORLD SERIES RECORD | | | | | | |
|------|------|---|-----|---|----|----|-----|------|
|      |      | G | AB | R | H | HR | RBI | BA |
| 1951 | New York | 2 | 5 | 1 | 1 | 0 | 0 | .200 |
| 1952 | New York | 7 | 29 | 5 | 10 | 2 | 3 | .345 |
| 1953 | New York | 6 | 24 | 3 | 5 | 2 | 7 | .208 |
| 1955 | New York | 3 | 10 | 1 | 2 | 1 | 1 | .200 |
| 1956 | New York | 7 | 24 | 6 | 6 | 3 | 4 | .250 |
| 1957 | New York | 6 | 19 | 3 | 5 | 1 | 2 | .263 |
| 1958 | New York | 7 | 24 | 4 | 6 | 2 | 3 | .250 |
| 1960 | New York | 7 | 25 | 8 | 10 | 3 | 11 | .400 |
| 1961 | New York | 2 | 6 | 0 | 1 | 0 | 0 | .167 |
| 1962 | New York | 7 | 25 | 2 | 3 | 0 | 0 | .120 |
| 1963 | New York | 4 | 15 | 1 | 2 | 1 | 1 | .133 |
| 1964 | New York | 7 | 24 | 8 | 8 | 3 | 8 | .333 |
| W.S. | Totals | 65 | 230 | 42 | 59 | 18 | 40 | .257 |

*Led league

## WILLIE, MICKEY, AND THE DUKE

|        | Years | Games | AB | R | H | HR | RBI | Ave. |
|--------|-------|-------|-----|-----|-----|-----|-------|------|
| **Mantle** | 18 | 2,401 | 8,102 | 1,677 | 2,415 | 536 | 1,509 | .298 |
| **Mays** | 22 | 2,992 | 10,881 | 2,062 | 3,283 | 660 | 1,903 | .302 |
| **Snider** | 18 | 2,143 | 7,161 | 1,259 | 2,116 | 407 | 1,333 | .295 |

# MICKEY MANTLE'S SELECTED READING LIST

(A collection of works and sources related to the New York Yankees, and my career, that were helpful in researching this book)

Allen, Maury. *Baseball's 100.* New York: A&W Publishers, 1981.

Cohen, Richard, and Neft, David. *The World Series.* New York: Collier Books, 1976.

Gallagher, Mark. *Explosion!* New York: Arbor House, 1987.

Houk, Ralph, and Creamer, Robert. *Season of Glory.* New York: G. P. Putnam's Sons, 1988.

Kubek, Tony, and Pluto, Jerry. *Sixty-One.* New York: Macmillan Publishing Co., 1987.

Mantle, Mickey, with Herb Gluck. *The Mick.* New York: Doubleday, 1985.

Nemec, David. *Great Baseball Feats, Facts & Firsts.* New York: Plume, 1987.

Peary, Danny, ed. *Cult Baseball Players.* New York: Fireside, 1990.

Rosenthal, Harold. *The 10 Best Years of Baseball.* Chicago: Contemporary Books, 1979.

Schiffer, Don. *World Series Encyclopedia.* New York: Thomas Nelson & Sons, 1961.

Thorn, John. *A Century of Baseball Lore.* New York: Hart Publishing Co., Inc., 1974.

**Newspapers and News Services**

Associated Press
*Brooklyn Eagle*
*New York Daily News*
*New York Herald-Tribune*
*New York Times*
SABR (Society for American Baseball Research)
Scripps-Howard News Service
*Sporting News*
*Sports Illustrated*
United Press

# INDEX